Career Success!

A Step-By-Step Workbook for Students, Job Seekers and Lifelong Learners

Third Edition

Urban G. Whitaker, Ph.D.

O'BRIEN & WHITAKER PUBLISHERS
P.O. Box 10973
Oakland, California 94610
phone/fax: 888.924.2658
email: office@obrienandwhitaker.com

CAREER SUCCESS! © 2002 Urban Whitaker
COVER ILLUSTRATION AND VIGNETTES © 2002 Bud Peen

All rights reserved. No part of this book may be used or reproduced in any manner without written permission from the publisher except in the case of quotations embodied in articles or reviews. The invitation to photocopy multiple copies of the Exercises contained in this book is for the personal use of the purchaser of the book. Bulk discounts for sale of the book to classes, etc. will be gladly given.

Produced by West Coast Print Center in the United States
ISBN 0-9668431-6-9

Table of Contents

A Note to Workbook Users 1

INTRODUCTION
Five Essential Steps to Career and Job Satisfaction 9

TASK ONE
Clarifying Your Values 15

EXERCISE 1
Identifying Your Career-Related Values
Worksheet: Identifying Your Values 19

EXERCISE 2
Prioritizing Your Career-Related Values
Worksheet: Your Values Priority Grid 29
International Career and Job Values 30

TASK TWO
Assessing Your Skills 34

EXERCISE 3
Rating Yourself on 76 Career-Transferable Skills
Worksheet: The Skills List 40

EXERCISE 4
Grouping Your Transferable Skills
Worksheet: Your Own Category Ratings 51

EXERCISE 5
Rating Your Transferable Skills
Worksheet: Your Skills Priority Grid   58

EXERCISES 6 & 7
Analyzing Your Skills in Action

EXERCISE 6
Looking At Your Strong Skills in Action
Worksheet: Examining the Strengths in Your
Transferable Skills Profile   63

EXERCISE 7
Looking At Your Weaker Skills in Action
Worksheet: Examining the Weaknesses in Your
Transferable Skills Profile   67

TASK THREE
Matching Your Profiles   69

EXERCISE 8
Conducting Information Interviews
Suggestions for Conducting
Information Interviews   74
Worksheet: Information Interview Data Sheet   78

TASK FOUR
Bridging the Gap   81
What is Your Learning Style?   82

EXERCISE 9
Identifying Your Learning Needs
Worksheet: Your Learning Needs Grid
and List of Learning Objectives   90

EXERCISE 10
Selecting Your Learning Activities and Resources
Worksheet: Learning Activities   94
Worksheet: Learning Resources   96

EXERCISE 11
Evaluating Your Progress
Worksheet: Evaluating Your Progress   102

EXERCISE 12
Completing Your Learning Plans
Worksheet: Learning Plan Summary   105

TASK FIVE
Sharpening Your Skills
Heredity, Luck and Influence: Three Wild Cards   108
Resumes and Job Interviews   111

EXERCISE 13
Creating Your Career Relevance Profile
Worksheet: Checklist #1: Traditional Learning   117
Worksheet: Checklist #2: Untranscripted Experiential Learning   119

EXERCISE 14
Writing Your Resume
Worksheet: Questions about the Form and Content of Resumes   128
Worksheet: Answers: What Kind of Resume Do You Prefer for Yourself?   129

EXERCISE 15
Preparing for Job Interviews   130
Worksheet: Possible Do's and Don'ts About Job Interviews   132
Worksheet: The Most Common Questions Asked in Job Interviews   134
Worksheet: Preparation for Successful Job Interviews   136
Interviewing Practice   137
Worksheet: Interview Practice and Rehearsal Plans   139
Job Success and Career Success   140

CONCLUSION
Learning to Learn: The Master Key   141

EXERCISE 16   Lifelong Learning Logs
Monitors of Your Career Success   142
Worksheet: The Lifelong Learning Log   145

APPENDICES: Helpful Resources   146
Job Search Strategies   146
International Jobs and Careers   146
Computerized Career Programs   147
Learning   149
Professional Organizations   150
About the Author   154

This book is dedicated to those who have been the most helpful contributors to its formula for career success

My Family and My Students

Acknowledgments

In the deepest sense, the creation of this workbook has been a cooperative endeavor. I have put it together. I am responsible for any errors or other weaknesses. But the credit for its strengths as a formula for career success must be shared widely.

As I indicated in the dedication, it is my family and my students who have made the greatest contribution to this work. All the members of my family have read and responded helpfully to the various drafts of this publication. My students in the career development courses I taught for twenty years at San Francisco State University have contributed hundreds of ideas and have tested all of the exercises in this workbook.

There is no way to adequately express my deep personal appreciation and my professional indebtedness to Morris Keeton. The dictionary defines "mentor" as a "wise and trusted counselor." Morris Keeton has been my mentor for more than three decades. Beyond the benefits of his personal counsel, his leadership as the founding President of CAEL (The Council for Adult and Experiential Learning) has enriched the resource base for all of us who have been fortunate enough to have him as a colleague.

I am indebted to CAEL and to the W.K. Kellogg Foundation of Battle Creek, Michigan for providing the resources and logistical support to establish The Learning Center in the 1970's and 80's.

I am particularly grateful to Paul Breen, my colleague and co-author of numerous educational resources including *Bridging the Gap* to which this workbook is a close relative. Paul was the primary developer of the list of 76 career-transferable skills, and of the values and skills grids that have been adapted from their original publication in 1981.

Marian O'Brien and Keith Whitaker have contributed a great deal more than can be adequately described as "production". They have given extensive help and advice on layout, organization and content in every part of the book. Elizabeth Whitaker has done an excellent job of coordinating the network of *Bridging the Gap* and *Career Success Workbook* users for several years and has organized the distribution for both books.

I am more indebted to all of those named in this brief acknowledgment than I can say in a few sentences. And, again, I want to express my special appreciation to all of my students and colleagues. They have contributed the best of what may be useful in this workbook.

Urban Whitaker
San Francisco

A Note to Workbook Users

This workbook is designed as a conversation with the users: lifelong learners of all ages from high school students who are choosing their first careers, to those who are seeking increased levels of success in their current jobs, to senior citizens considering a career change. As you begin this process, ask yourself not whether you *can* become a more effective lifelong learner, but how you *will*.

Whether you are working alone or in a group we believe that it is possible for you to greatly improve your chances for career success by completing the Tasks and Exercises in this book from start to finish. However, we are quick to agree that each of us has our own personal approach to learning and that you may decide to undertake these exercises in a different order than the one we have chosen. You may also find it useful to include an exercise or activity from another career planning source. Your career success depends on your ability to discover and utilize all available resources that work for you.

Lifelong Learning

You *are* a lifelong learner. Your effectiveness as a lifelong learner will be the most important factor in determining your career success.

Lifelong learning is not new. What *is* new is the growing realization among employers, employees, teachers and trainers that mid-career learning is as important to career success as the learning you acquired in school or college. As the vital role of lifelong learning became more obvious a Commission for a Nation of Lifelong Learners was created in 1995. The Commission was funded by the Kellogg Foundation and made its first report on its findings at a national conference in Washington, D.C. in November of 1997. Since that time, the term lifelong learning has become commonplace.

What does lifelong learning mean to your personal search for career success? It may once have been true that for most working people life had three main phases: *1. learning*, from birth through the end of formal schooling; *2. working*, at a career or job for which the learning was intended as basic preparation; and *3. retirement*.

Even the possibility of such a neat three-stage life has all but disappeared. Twelve or more years of preparation is no longer a sufficient foundation for career success. Now even those earning advanced degrees for specific careers, must plan to pursue continuing education activities throughout their working lives.

This will mean keeping up with journals and professional publications, attending conferences and workshops, or taking seminars or formal courses. For people in all kinds of careers, it means being ready to learn from *experience* on a daily basis.

It can easily be seen why effective lifelong learning is a prerequisite to career success. Technological, sociological and other changes simply happen too fast and too unpredictably to permit us to draw a sharp line between preparing for a career and succeeding in it. As a lifelong learner, what knowledge do you need for success, and how can you acquire the skills you'll benefit the most from?

Experiential Learning

You are not only a *lifelong* learner, but a lifelong *experiential* learner. For career success in the rapidly changing environment of the twenty-first century you will need to sharpen both your *traditional* learning skills, (learning from books, and in classrooms) and your *experiential* learning skills (learning on-the-job and through independent study activities).

It will be important for you to know what kind of learner you are. Most of us learn best through a particular personal combination of traditional and experiential learning activities. We urge you to take advantage of the many available instruments for determining what your personal learning style is. On page 83 we describe one of these resources, the Kolb *Learning Styles Inventory*.

Learning Organizations   In the Appendix we have described a number of organizations that specialize in various aspects of lifelong experiential learning. They offer a wide range of useful and proven resources, as well as membership opportunities for institutions and individuals.

Alternative Degree Programs   All of the alternative degree programs recognize the value of experiential learning and emphasize the importance of combining classroom learning with learning on-the-job. Most of them also provide ways for you to assess your prior experiential learning—the college-level learning which you may have acquired from previous work or other experience.

Prior Learning Assessment   CAEL (The Council for Adult and Experiential Learning) has published a best-selling book by Lois Lamdin, *Earn College Credit for What You Know,* now in its third edition, which describes the process of prior learning assessment. CAEL also publishes another excellent resource entitled *Prior Learning Assessment: A Guidebook to American Institutional Practices,* that lists more than 1000 colleges and universities that grant credit for prior learning and how that learning is assessed. (See CAEL publications on pg. 149.)

Internships   In career counseling there is near unanimity about the importance of internships. An internship is a trial run that will give you your very best opportunity to see whether a particular career is right for you. Both parties are well-served. You get to test the waters; your temporary employer gets your services, usually at comparatively low cost, and gets a chance to evaluate you as a prospective employee.

Internships vary in a number of ways:

Terminology Some are called internships and some are called externships. Some don't actually have a name, but are variations of "field experience" assignments in educational institutions. (See next page for a description of cooperative education.)

Duration Internships may vary from a few months to as long as a year. Some are part-time and others are full-time.

Pay Some are unpaid; others offer stipends that vary from "expenses" to minimum wage, or even to apprentice level salaries.

Credit Some internships include formal arrangements for academic credit.

Role Some interns are given only routine "busy work" duties; others get opportunities to perform at higher levels of responsibility.

Obviously, you will need to be careful to get an internship that fits your own personal needs. Whatever the arrangements, however, the most important function of an internship is the opportunity to see whether or not you like a particular career or job environment, and whether or not you are able to do well in it.

When testing a work environment to see whether it matches your values and skills profiles you will need to distinguish between those factors that are career-specific and those that may be characteristic only of a particular job within the career. For example, if the internship proves to be a high stress experience, is it stressful because of the type of work (career-related stress) or because of the particular supervisor or colleagues or other environmental factors in the workplace (job-related stress).

Cooperative Education   This differs from "internships" in a number of ways. Most importantly it is often full-time work alternated with full-time school. A cooperative education formally integrates a student's academic and/or career interests with productive work experience in cooperating employer organizations. This form of education can function at the high school level as well as the college level. The National Commission for Cooperative Education has an extensive website at www.co-op.edu that addresses how co-op works to the student's benefit and lists the colleges and businesses that currently participate in the program.

Career-Transferable Skills

Because you may have more than one career and will very likely have more than one job within each career, a very special importance is attached to career and job-transferable skills. The centerpiece of this book is a list of 76 career-transferable skills. (*Exercise 3*, p. 39) This list was developed in discussions with hundreds of employers, employees and teachers. We asked employers what skills they most wanted their employees to have. We asked employees what skills they thought were contributing to their career success. We asked the faculty members what transferable skills might be developed in their high school and college classes. Millions of these lists have been completed and put to beneficial use by career seekers during the last 20 years.

We urge you to pay special attention to Skill #24: "Analyze and learn from life experience. This "learning to learn" skill is the master skill of all the transferable skills.

Tips on Using this Workbook

Before you begin working in the book, we suggest you make extra copies of each of the worksheets you will be using when completing the 16 Exercises. These will be useful for revisions, for job-specific alternate versions and for corrections.

Write notes in the margins. They are generous for that purpose. "Dog-ear" pages that you find yourself going back to. Use your highlighter freely.

Consider beginning a Lifelong Learning Journal now using copies of the sheets provided for Exercise 16 on pg. 145. You might also begin a separate book that you can keep handy for taking notes or expanding on the lists in this book. You will benefit greatly from regular reporting on your progress and career-related issues.

This book contains a formula for success. It assumes that you must have five essential ingredients for job and career satisfaction:

1.) a clear set of values

2.) an accurate assessment of your present skills

3.) a career that is a good match for your values and skills profiles

4.) an effective lifelong learning plan to help you bridge the gap between your present skills and those you will need for career success

5.) good job-seeking skills.

Note: Throughout this book we have alternated the use of gender-specific terms and although the book has a single author, it is narrated as the plural "we" because all of the Tasks and Exercises in the book have been developed with the help of many students, teachers, employees and employers.

We have used the five-part formula in this workbook in many classes and workshops over the past twenty-plus years. We know from the responses of our students and individual users that they themselves have been the primary ingredients in the determination of success in their careers.

We wish you a lifetime of career success!

INTRODUCTION
Five Essential Steps to Career and Job Satisfaction

The purpose of this workbook is to give you the tools you need to be successful in your career and satisfied with your job. We have developed five basic tasks to help you toward career success:

TASK ONE is deciding what you do and don't like about work. These are your "values." The purpose of Task One is to develop your Values Profile. When you finish it you will have a clearer picture of what you want in a career.

TASK TWO is to develop your Skills Profile by identifying your levels of proficiency on a list of 76 career-transferable skills.

TASK THREE is to match your personal values and skills profiles to the most appropriate career for you—to make sure that you are not one of the eight out of ten people who are in the wrong job.

TASK FOUR is to develop a learning plan for you to bridge the gap between your present skills profile and the skills you will need for success in the career of your choice.

TASK FIVE is to sharpen your job-seeking skills — particularly resume writing and interviewing — so that you can win the job assignments you will need for a successful career.

As you work on these five tasks you will be completing fifteen exercises. Additionally, there is one final exercise that we have included as a sort of "career success insurance policy." This last exercise is an outline for writing Lifelong Learning Logs. The logs are designed to support continuing efficiency in your on-the-job learning.

Before you get started with this workbook it is important to decide exactly what the word "career" means to you. Because so many people use "job" and "career" interchangeably you will need to know not only what those terms mean to you, but also what they sometimes mean to others who use them differently. And, for those who wish to have *international* career success, it is important to distinguish between "international" and "foreign" since those terms also mean different things to different people.

Is it a "Job" or is it a "Career"?

In this workbook we make a clear distinction between a career and a job. A career is what *kind* of work you do; a job is a particular arrangement between you and an employer. A career is *what* you do, and a job is *where* and *for whom* you do it.

We believe that career and job can be synonymous. In other words we believe that it is possible, and certainly desirable, that what you are doing for your employer is exactly what you want to be doing in your career. It is likely that many of the eight out of ten people who are in the wrong job are dissatisfied because their jobs are not in the same field as their preferred careers. For example, a person who drives a taxi as her job, may actually prefer a career in writing. In many cases jobs are pursued simply to make a living, while the worker's real desire is to pursue a career in another field. The happiest people at work are those whose jobs are central to their careers. For example, one whose chosen career is education may be happy in a series of jobs as a teacher or administrator in different institutions.

Defined in this way the following are examples of *careers:* education, music, medicine, business, journalism, politics, food service, etc.

Among the many different kinds of *jobs* within each of these career fields might be:

    teacher in an elementary school (or administrator in a high school or college);

drummer in a band (or conductor of a major symphony);

lab technician at a hospital (or nurse, or cardiac surgeon);

salesperson for a manufacturing firm (or Chief Executive Officer);

proofreader for a publishing company (or a published author);

City Council Member (or Member of Congress);

waitperson at a restaurant (or owner-chef).

Success and satisfaction depend on two things: first, being in the right career (*i.e.*, doing the kind of thing you like to do); and second, being in the right job (*i.e.*, performing your work for the right people in the right environment). In this workbook we will address both of these essential ingredients for success. In the first chapter your task is to decide what you would like to do as a career. In the last chapter your task will be to develop your job-seeking skills to find the right combination of jobs that will provide the foundation for your success.

Suggestion: Before you begin to work on your Values Profile, write out your own personal definitions of "job" and "career." To get a helpful perspective on these definitions we suggest that you conduct an informal poll. Ask your family, friends and acquaintances whether they consider their work to be a job or a career, or both. Consider your own employment history. Is the work you are doing, or have done, only a job, or could it be considered a part of your career? If you aren't completely satisfied with your work is it because you are not in the right career — that is, doing the kind of thing you really like to do, or are you, perhaps, in the right career, but in the wrong job?

What is your definition of:

job _____

_____

_____

_____

_____

_____

_____

_____

career _____

_____

_____

_____

_____

_____

_____

_____

Your own employment history: jobs/careers?

_____
_____
_____
_____
_____
_____
_____
_____
_____
_____
_____
_____

International Careers

If you would like to have an international career it is important for you to develop two more personalized definitions: "international" and "foreign." As with the definitions of job and career there are no universally accepted definitions for either of these terms. Often they are used interchangeably. The important thing is for you to know what the label "international career" means to you and to be alert to the fact that other people may not use the same definition.

In the most technical sense "international" refers to activities involving more than one nation-state. "Foreign" refers to activities within one nation-state other than your own. Some people who seek international careers are mostly interested in living and working in another country. For example, an American teacher may wish to spend some years teaching in Spain. Is that an international career? It depends. If the teacher is in an American school in Madrid teaching the children of American service personnel with the same lesson plans that are used in Chicago, then it may be a "foreign job." The teacher is pursuing a career in a foreign place. But it isn't necessarily "international." On the other hand, the teacher might actually pursue an international career without ever leaving Chicago if he teaches a foreign language to American students who are planning to go overseas, or if he teaches foreign exchange students.

As you develop your Values Profile it will be very important for you to know what it is about an international career that is attractive to you. Is it working with people of other cultures? Is it traveling, living or working in one or more other cultures? Is it participating in certain kinds of activities such as promoting intercultural understanding or developing international law?

In some respects almost all careers are international. It is difficult to imagine very many kinds of work that do not, in some way, involve people or products from more than one culture.

What would interest you in an international career?

TASK ONE
Clarifying Your Values

What are values? Why is values clarification essential to career success? Perhaps the best way to answer these questions is with examples. Some of the most common career-related values are: money, prestige, leisure and contribution to improvements in society. To get a start on clarifying your career values, ask yourself whether any or all of these four values are important to you. And then try to put them in the order of their importance. One person may say that her single most important career value is making a lot of money. She may not really care too much about whether her career contributes to social progress. Another person may get more satisfaction from contributing to the improvement of society, and be willing to accept a lower income.

The first step is to discover what your own values are.

EXERCISE 1
Identifying Your Career-Related Values

Making a list of your values is not as easy as it might seem. There are many more career-related values than the four that are mentioned above. All of us have many values and they are so much a part of us that we aren't always aware of them as values. For that reason we strongly advise you to undertake this exercise in two steps. *First,* make a list of all the possible career-related values that you can imagine. *Second,* select from this list all of the values that seem relevant to your own happiness in a career.

A very strong benefit of this Exercise lies in clarifying the essence of your own values. Our values have come to us through our families, our neighborhoods, our religions and our cultures. By carrying out this Exercise you will refine the journey of discovery, distilling and further defining what makes up your own values profile.

Suggestion: Once you have made your comprehensive list, we recommend one of two paths: if you are studying career development in a group it may be most effective to have each member make a list independently, then to discuss each list and combine them to maximize the number of possible values. If you are undertaking this task alone as a self-directed learner it will be very helpful if you talk to several people about the things that they like and don't like in their jobs or careers.

Once you have developed a large list of possible career-related values you can pare it down to the list of values that are important to you personally. As you create this preliminary list it is a good idea to double check your selections with someone who knows you well. It is also helpful to test the list against your own experience — remembering which work-related activities have been most satisfying to you, and which have been less enjoyable.

Worksheet for Exercise 1: Identifying Your Values

Instructions: The Values List on p. 20 is only a small sample of the more complete list from which you will want to select your own important values. *First*, complete the list, making it as large as you (and any who are working with you) can make it. *Second*, select values from it for your own list. There is no magic number of values that should be transferred from the complete list to your own preliminary list of important values on p. 21. You may want to start with 20 or more values that are important to you. In any case we recommend that you choose at least a dozen to begin with. Later, in *Exercise 2*, you will be rating and ranking your most important values.

Sample Values List

complete this list with as many additional values as you can

Economic Security	**Others**
making money	_____
health benefits	_____
vacation	_____
retirement benefits	_____
	_____
Workplace Conditions	_____
physical security	_____
congenial colleagues	_____
location	_____
hours of work	_____
avoiding stress	_____
	_____
Your Role	_____
making decisions	_____
supervising others	_____
prestige	_____
	_____
Social Impact of Career	_____
environmental conservation	_____
helping the underprivileged	_____
improving race relations	_____
	_____
Personal Preferences	_____
challenging work	_____
competition	_____
working alone	_____
	_____

Your Preliminary Values List

select the values from the sample list that are important to you (select at least 12)

1. _____
2. _____
3. _____
4. _____
5. _____
6. _____
7. _____
8. _____
9. _____
10. _____
11. _____
12. _____
13. _____
14. _____
15. _____
16. _____
17. _____
18. _____
19. _____
20. _____
21. _____
22. _____
23. _____

EXERCISE 2
Prioritizing Your Career-Related Values

Remember that the primary purpose of developing an accurate Values Profile is to set the stage for selecting a career in which you will be happy. For that reason it is very important to decide which values are the most important to you and to put that list of values in priority order. One way of determining this priority order is to ask yourself which of your values are so important that you simply would not consider a career, or a job, in which those values would not be satisfied. For example, if your family life is so important to you that you would not ever want to be away from home for more than a day or two you might decide not to be a politician, or a foreign correspondent, or a traveling salesperson. Or, if avoiding daily stress is an absolutely top value for you, you may decide that you could never be a television news anchor, or an FBI agent, or the manager of an athletic team. If these examples applied to you, you would rate them of highest importance and would plot them in the #10 vertical column to the far right on the grid as F and B are placed on the Sample Grid on pg. 27.

Another purpose of *Exercise 2* is to identify the degree to which some of your values may depend on further learning in order to maximize the probability that you will be able to satisfy them. Notice on the

Sample Grid, for example, that Value "B" (Avoiding Stress) is placed near the bottom on the #2 horizontal line. This indicates that the Sample Learner doesn't believe that the avoidance of career stress depends much on further learning. Value "F" (marriage and family) is placed at the extreme bottom of the scale for the same reason. Notice, however, that this placement is a matter of personal judgment. One might argue that the more learning you have, the more likely you are to be able to "write your own ticket" (*i.e.*, to succeed in a career or a job of your choice that fits your values profile).

Some values, however, more clearly require specific learning. For example, if the value is "to work in France or Japan" then some foreign language learning will be required to maximize the chances of satisfying that value. Still the proper place for that value in the vertical dimension of the grid depends on the individual learner's current competence. Someone who is already fully proficient in the appropriate foreign language might place that value at or near the bottom of the grid (*e.g.*, column 10, line 1), for even though it is essential to have significant learning it has already been acquired.

Paradoxes

Some values may be held very highly, yet not be very meaningful on the Values Grid unless they are broken down into their component parts. A prime example is the value "satisfying." Many people say that "satisfaction" is their primary career value. You may feel very strongly that you will not choose a career unless you are convinced that it will be satisfying to you. That is a very important fact to know, but it serves more as a question than as an answer when you are trying to decide what career to enter. In fact, the whole purpose of this workbook is to help you to find a satisfying career. It just won't help you very much to put "satisfying" on your grid in the #10 column on the right hand side. What will help is to be more specific about your values by answering the question: "What will be satisfying to me?" Your answer, for example, may be "a career that: 1.) pays well; 2.) involves extensive travel; 3.) is prestigious; 4.) contributes to environmental conservation; etc." Once you have identified these more specific components of the umbrella value "satisfying" then you can place each of them at appropriate places on the Values Grid. What you will have is: *first,* a useful priority order of your values which will enable you to find the most satisfying career; and *second,* an accurate indication of additional learning goals you should seek in order to maximize your chances of career satisfaction.

This same paradox — a value that is extremely important, yet would put questions rather than answers on your grid — applies not only to umbrella values like "satisfaction" and "happiness" but to several others. For example, if you want a career that is "challenging" or "exciting" you will need to treat these, too, as questions: *What* is challenging or exciting to you? The answers will help you to identify the specific values that are most essential to include in a values profile. The same pattern applies to overarching values such as preference for "intellectually stimulating work" or a "creative career environment." The key values questions are: "What do you find to be intellectually stimulating? What are the characteristics of an environment that seems appropriately creative to you?

Values are Personal

There is nothing that is absolutely right or wrong about most values. Nobody can tell you, for example, that "travel" is intrinsically a good value. For one person the accurate description of the travel-related value is "I want a career that maximizes the opportunities for travel." For another, the accurate description may be: "I am a homebody and I must have a career that does not require me to travel." The same thing is true about "hours of work." Some people want to avoid the rigidity of a nine-to-five routine; others prefer the predictability of an arrangement that enables them to leave the career at the office when the clock strikes five. Similarly "location" may be an important value. But to one person that means being in a big city; another may prefer the quiet atmosphere and more casual life of a small town or rural setting.

In contrast to variable values such as travel, working hours and location there are the more black-and-white, yes-or-no values such as a good benefits package, contributing to environmental improvement and having congenial colleagues. These kinds of values may be higher or lower on your list, but hardly anyone positively wishes to avoid benefits, or to worsen the environment or to have nasty colleagues. Unlike "travel" which may be a definite plus or a definite minus, values like benefits and environmental conservation have only plus grades. The meaning, for you, of the differences in these kinds of values questions is simply that you need to be specific about both the definition of each value and about the degree of its importance to you. If the values question is "travel" your answer needs to be either "yes" or "no" and, if yes, how much. If the values question is "creative work environment" you need to be specific about what things you consider to be creative, as well as how important each of them is to you. If the value is "money" you probably need to translate it into the things that money can buy: location and quality of housing; type and number of automobiles (boats, airplanes); frequency, length and types of vacations; and other elements of living style. With telecommuting and other distance work arrangements, it is increasingly possible to find many different ways to strike the balance between cost-of-living and the size of your paycheck. Although it may be somewhat helpful to know how important "money" is to you in the abstract, it will be much more useful if your values profile is specific about the role of the things money can buy.

Sample Values Priority Grid

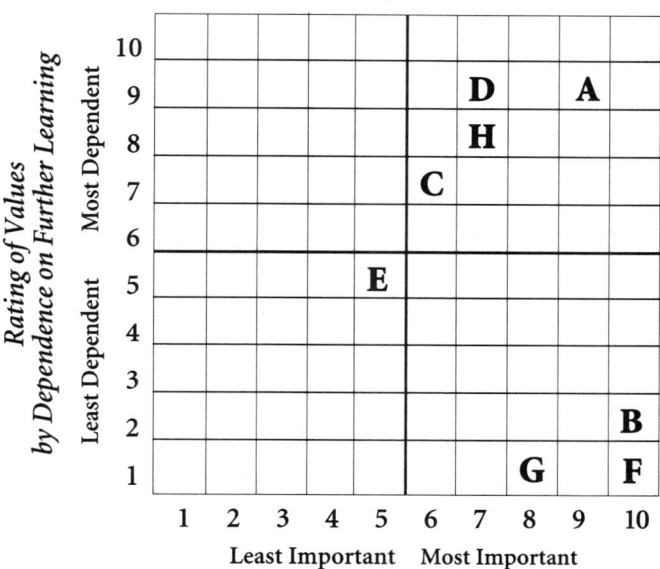

Sample List of Values	Importance to You	Dependence on Further Learning
A. making money	9	9
B. avoiding stress	10	2
C. travel	6	7
D. making decisions	7	9
E. public service	5	5
F. marriage/family	10	1
G. honesty/integrity	8	1
H. independence	7	8

Worksheet for Exercise 2: Your Values Priority Grid

Instructions:

Step 1. Return to *Exercise 1* (pg. 21) and select the eight values that are the most important to you.

Step 2. Make sure that each value is stated specifically enough to be useful. You may want to revise your list if you find values that are too vague or generic. Enter your eight values in any order, on the lettered lines provided at the bottom of pg. 29.

Step 3. When you have selected the eight specific values that are most important to you, rate each one independently on a scale of 1 to 10 — "1" being the least important and "10" the most — then enter that rating in the first column to the right of the listed value. Two or more values may have the same rating.

Step 4. Next, rate each of them according to the degree to which you believe they require further learning to maximize the probability that they will be satisfied. A "1" indicates little learning required; a "10" indicates considerable learning required. Enter the rating in the second column to the right of the list of values.

Step 5. Now each of your eight most important values has two ratings: a number from 1 to 10 indicating its importance to you; and another indicating its dependence on further learning. Plot them on your personal Values Grid at the top of pg. 29.

Your Values Priority Grid

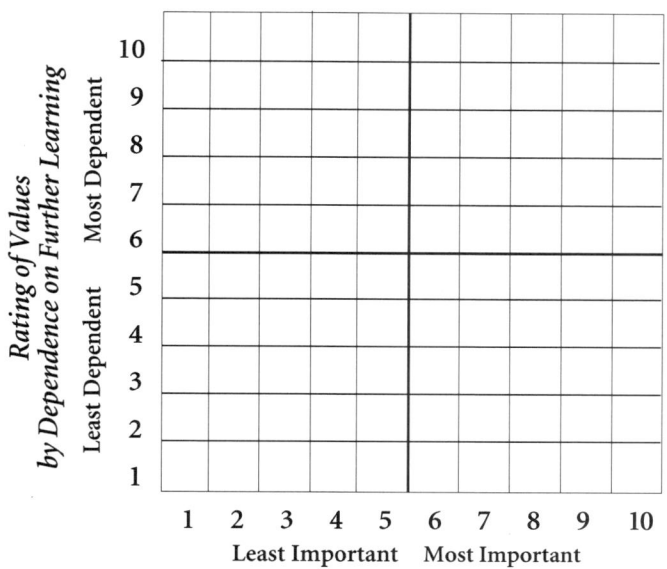

	Your List of Values	Importance to You	Dependence on Further Learning
A.	_____		
B.	_____		
C.	_____		
D.	_____		
E.	_____		
F.	_____		
G.	_____		
H.	_____		

Using the Values Profile

Remember that the purpose of these exercises is to enhance your career success. The values profile will help you in two ways: *first*, in selecting a career, you will be wise to pay special attention to the right hand half of the Grid — those values that you have ranked in the top five categories of importance; *second*, in preparing for your career you will want to pay special attention to the top half of the Grid — those values areas which are most likely to be satisfied only if you seek some additional learning.

When you get to *Task Three: Matching Your Profiles*, in this workbook, you will be using the right hand side of your Grid, putting care-ful attention to the fit between your Values Profile and potential careers. When you get to *Task Four: Bridging the Gap* you will want to give special attention to the top half of your Values Grid — those values which you believe can benefit from further learning.

International Career and Job Values

Most values are as relevant in international careers or jobs as they are in the domestic work environment. Some values, however, are particularly affected by foreign or international career activities. Among the most obvious are travel, family and intercultural values.

Foreign Travel and Residence

Not all international careers or jobs require travel. However, if you do desire to travel and work outside your own country it will probably be an international career or job almost by definition. The most common problem (but it is by no means insurmountable) will be for those who want international careers, but who, for family or other reasons, wish to avoid travel. Fortunately there are many international careers and jobs that involve little or no travel and do not require residence abroad.

Family-Related Values

International careers may have either positive or negative impacts on family life depending not only on the particular career, but also on differences in values. For example, travel and residence abroad may be viewed as a very positive opportunity by those who value the chance for themselves and their children to learn foreign languages and experience foreign cultures. On the other hand, some people may not put a high value on this opportunity and may feel negative about being so far away from the familiar home environment.

Moving around a lot (as in the diplomatic or military services) is viewed positively by some who enjoy frequent change and making new friends. Others may see constant changes as being negative for such reasons as having to leave old friends behind, changing children's schools, moving belongings, etc. In your evaluations of your Values Priority Grid, you will want to very carefully consider your responses, and your family's, if appropriate, to these considerations.

Intercultural Interactions

Whether or not your international career involves travel or residence abroad it will involve some degree of interaction with people of other cultures. Unless this is a positive value for you it is probably not a good idea to consider an international career. A major advantage (to some) or disadvantage (to others) about many international careers is the need to learn and use one or more foreign languages. And also as vital will be the need to educate yourself about the various cultures you will be in contact with. By learning what a specific culture's values are, you will be aiming towards success in business and personal interactions with the people from that culture.

As with almost any career, the values served or denied will vary considerably from job to job within the same career. There are many emerging international career opportunities. In general it is fair to say that international careers offer at least as many positive outcomes as domestic careers. For those who enjoy challenge, variety and the opportunity to influence the development of the world community, an international career may be a very good way to go.

Changes in Values

One last note before you proceed to *Task 2: Assessing Your Skills*. Your values may change, and your *perceptions* of your values may change. Between now and the time it takes you to get to *Task 3: Matching Your Profiles*, you may have some new thoughts about the ways in which you described and prioritized your values originally. If so, you will want to review and perhaps revise your Values Grid.

Actual changes in your values (as distinct from mere changes in your perceptions of them) may occur over a longer period. It may be helpful to your long-term career success if you review your values profile periodically. Keeping a Lifelong Learning Journal, as suggested earlier, can make this review process much easier and add depth to the results.

"Mid-career change" has become a familiar phrase in the contemporary vocabulary. Some estimates suggest that the average person will have as many as 5 to 7 careers in a lifetime. The most important thing for your career success and satisfaction is that you always maintain a compatible relationship between your values and your career — a relationship that develops and changes as you do.

TASK TWO
Assessing Your Skills

There are two important reasons why you need an accurate inventory of your skills:

> 1.) you need to know your strengths so that you can make the career choices that best suit your abilities;
>
> 2.) you need to know your weaknesses so that you can avoid career mismatches.

A clear and accurate assessment of your skills profile will also serve two other important purposes: your strengths will provide excellent content for your resume as well as important discussion points for your job interviews. In addition, your weaker skill areas can be re-cast as learning objectives to be included in your self-directed learning plan (*Task 4* in this workbook).

To provide maximum benefit, your completed skills inventory must reflect an accurate and clear image of your current strengths and weaknesses.

This will be a good place for you to make multiple copies of the Career-Transferable Skills worksheets. Do the list once through, fairly quickly, then put it aside and return to it later. Think carefully about your first responses. Are they accurate? Do they really fit you currently? Do the list again. Talk with others who know you well. See if they arrive at the same answers that you did.

Career-Relevant Strengths

Before you complete your career development activities you will find it very helpful to consider three different kinds of strengths. Two of them can be described as skills:

• Some of the most important skills are career-transferable, *i.e.,* they contribute to success in many different kinds of careers. In *Exercises 3-6* you will be assessing these skills.

• The other branch of your skills profile encompasses job-specific skills. They are not covered in the assessment exercises in this workbook because, by definition, they vary for each different career or job. After you have finished *Task 3: Matching Your Profiles,* you will have some idea of your job-specific skill needs. Many employers, particularly for entry level positions, prefer to handle the development of job-specific skills with on-the-job training after you are hired.

The third important source of strengths that contribute to career success are such personal characteristics as motivation, congeniality, energy, empathy and a wide range of abilities that contribute to interpersonal effectiveness and work efficiency. It is very hard to draw a sharp line between these characteristics and "skills." Indeed we have blurred that line in a number of places in the list of 76 career-transferable skills. For example, Skill #49 ("Understanding the feelings of others") is an aspect of empathy. While empathy may be described as a skill, its sources are deeply rooted in personality characteristics that result more from the influences of family life than from classroom learning. An important clue to whether a strength is properly called a skill is the answer to the question, can it be learned? It is possible to improve your effectiveness in understanding others, yet some people are just more naturally empathetic.

It isn't important to pursue the debate on definition. What is important is for you to know your strengths, whether they are called skills or personal characteristics. Whenever you lack a strength that you need for career success you will need to make a personal judgement about whether it is a skill that you can acquire or a weakness that you will need to work around.

The 76 Career-Transferable Skills

The list of skills that you will be assessing in *Exercise 3* was developed over a period of three years of intensive research and discussion. The list was reviewed and revised many times in response to workshops and conferences with groups of employers, employees, students and faculty members. Since the list was first published in 1981 it has been reprinted in many publications, both in the business world and in education. We encourage you to consider it as only the first step in defining the transferable skills that will affect your career success.

- It is worth every extra effort to be sure that you get an accurate assessment of your strengths and weaknesses. To avoid over or underrating yourself, we recommend that you allow *plenty* of time to complete and review your self-assessment of the 76 skills. When you have finished we suggest that you re-check each skill rating. When you are satisfied with your ratings, we strongly recommend that you discuss your skills profile with someone who knows you well. You might even want to have that person fill out the entire exercise — rating *you* — before you compare and discuss your ratings. For best results, both of you should identify specific experiences or situations that illustrate some of your skill strengths or that reflect some of your weaker performance areas. *Exercises 6 and 7* are designed specifically for this purpose and you may wish to preview them before completing this step.

- Your ratings may vary widely depending on the particular career that you have in mind as you rate your skills. For example, look at Skill #53: "Teach a skill, concept or principle to others." You may rate yourself "B" or even higher if the career you have in mind is in some area of business or government in which there is comparatively little need for a teaching skill. You might even anticipate that, as an entry level worker, you will more likely be the student than the teacher. On the other hand, if you are considering a career as a college professor you may decide to rate yourself as a "C" or even lower.

Similarly, you may vary your assessment standards as you think of different stages of a career. For example, look at Skill #70: "Motivate and lead people." If you are rating yourself for an entry level position with little or no requirement for leadership, you may quite properly consider that your skills in this area are satisfactory or better. But, if you are rating yourself in terms of your future aspirations to have an executive position your rating may be lower, recognizing that you need further development to reach the skill levels that will be required at the peak of your career.

As you approach *Exercise 3* it may be helpful for you to decide in advance what career, and what stage of that career, you are assuming as you rate your skill levels. As we mentioned earlier, consider your first round on *Exercise 3* to be a first draft rather than a final product. Remember to make additional copies of the skills assessment worksheets so that you can repeat and revise them as needed.

EXERCISE 3
Rating Yourself on 76 Career-Transferable Skills

Instructions: Read carefully each of the five rating scale definitions described below. For each of the 76 skills circle the letter on the rating scale that best indicates your level of proficiency in performing or applying each skill in specific situations. The first two rating scale categories, "A" and "B", indicate a skill strength. "A" denotes a very high proficiency — great enough to teach or assess that skill. "B" means that your performance level is commendable. The middle rating, "C", signifies a satisfactory level of proficiency. Level " D" indicates a weak, but developing skill and "E" implies a lack of skill.

At the end of this rating exercise you will arrange the 76 skills into nine groups that you may find easier to use for reference in writing your resume and preparing for job interviews. However, we recommend that you first complete the skills inventory which provides 76 individual performance indicators. By conscientiously completing this exercise you will get a comprehensive assessment of your transferable skill strengths and weaknesses.

Skill Description	Your Rating
1. Listen with objectivity and paraphrase the content of a message.	A B C D E
2. Use various forms and styles of written communication.	A B C D E
3. Speak effectively to individuals and groups.	A B C D E
4. Use various audio and visual media to present ideas.	A B C D E
5. Express your needs, wants, opinions and preferences without offending the sensitivities of others.	A B C D E
6. Identify and communicate value judgments effectively.	A B C D E
7. Describe objects or events with a minimum of factual errors.	A B C D E
8. Convey a positive self-image to others.	A B C D E
9. Use a variety of sources of information.	A B C D E
10. Apply a variety of methods to test the validity of data.	A B C D E

A=Very High Proficiency   B=Commendable
C=Satisfactory   D=Developing   E=Lacking

Skill Description   Your Rating

11. Identify problems and needs.   A   B   C   D   E

12. Design an experiment, plan or model that systematically defines a problem.   A   B   C   D   E

13. Identify information sources appropriate to special needs or problems.   A   B   C   D   E

14. Formulate questions relevant to clarifying a particular problem, topic or issue.   A   B   C   D   E

15. Identify quickly and accurately the critical issues when making a decision or solving a problem.   A   B   C   D   E

16. Identify a general principle that explains interrelated experiences or factual data.   A   B   C   D   E

17. Define the parameters of a problem.   A   B   C   D   E

18. Identify reasonable criteria for assessing the value or appropriateness of action or behavior.   A   B   C   D   E

19. Adapt your concepts and behavior to changing conventions or norms.   A   B   C   D   E

A=Very High Proficiency   B=Commendable
C=Satisfactory   D=Developing   E=Lacking

Skill Description   Your Rating

Skill Description	Your Rating
20. Apply appropriate criteria to strategies and action plans.	A B C D E
21. Take given premises and reason to their conclusion.	A B C D E
22. Create innovative solutions to complex problems.	A B C D E
23. Analyze the interrelationships of events and ideas from several perspectives.	A B C D E
24. Analyze and learn from life experiences — both your own and those of others.	A B C D E
25. Relate the skills developed in one environment (*e.g.,* school) to the requirements of another environment (*e.g.,* work).	A B C D E
26. Match knowledge about your own characteristics and abilities to information about job and career opportunities.	A B C D E
27. Identify, describe and assess the relative importance of your needs, values, interests, strengths and weaknesses.	A B C D E

A=Very High Proficiency   B=Commendable
C=Satisfactory   D=Developing   E=Lacking

Skill Description   Your Rating

Skill	Rating
28. Identify and use personal growth goals and strategies that are motivating.	A B C D E
29. Identify and describe skills acquired through formal education and general life experience.	A B C D E
30. Identify your own strengths and weaknesses.	A B C D E
31. Accept and learn from negative criticism.	A B C D E
32. Persist with a project when faced with failure unless it is clear that the project cannot be carried out or is not worth the time or effort needed to complete it.	A B C D E
33. Recognize when a project cannot be carried out or is not worth the time or effort to complete it.	A B C D E
34. Generate trust and confidence in others.	A B C D E
35. Take risks.	A B C D E
36. Accept the consequences of your own actions.	A B C D E

A=Very High Proficiency   B=Commendable
C=Satisfactory   D=Developing   E=Lacking

Skill Description	Your Rating
37. Represent yourself effectively to prospective employers.	A B C D E
38. Sort data and objects.	A B C D E
39. Compile and rank information.	A B C D E
40. Apply information to the solution of a specific problem or task.	A B C D E
41. Synthesize facts, concepts and principles.	A B C D E
42. Understand and use organizing principles.	A B C D E
43. Evaluate information against standards.	A B C D E
44. Guide a group toward achievement of a common goal.	A B C D E
45. Maintain group cooperation and support.	A B C D E
46. Delegate tasks and responsibilities.	A B C D E
47. Interact effectively with peers, superiors and subordinates.	A B C D E

A=Very High Proficiency   B=Commendable
C=Satisfactory   D=Developing   E=Lacking

Skill Description   Your Rating

Skill	Rating
48. Express your feelings properly.	A B C D E
49. Understand the feelings of others.	A B C D E
50. Use argumentation techniques to persuade others.	A B C D E
51. Make commitments to others.	A B C D E
52. Be willing to take risks.	A B C D E
53. Teach a skill, concept or principle to others.	A B C D E
54. Analyze behavior of self and others in group situations.	A B C D E
55. Demonstrate effective social behavior in a variety of settings and under different circumstances.	A B C D E
56. Work under time and environmental pressures.	A B C D E
57. Identify alternative courses of action.	A B C D E
58. Set realistic goals.	A B C D E

A=Very High Proficiency   B=Commendable
C=Satisfactory   D=Developing   E=Lacking

Skill Description	Your Rating
59. Follow through with a plan or decision.	A B C D E
60. Manage time efficiently and effectively.	A B C D E
61. Predict future trends and patterns.	A B C D E
62. Accommodate multiple demands for commitment of time, energy and resources.	A B C D E
63. Assess needs.	A B C D E
64. Make and keep a schedule.	A B C D E
65. Set priorities.	A B C D E
66. Analyze tasks.	A B C D E
67. Identify people who can contribute to the solution of a problem or completion of a task.	A B C D E
68. Identify resource materials useful in the solution of a problem.	A B C D E
69. Delegate responsibility for completion of a task.	A B C D E

A=Very High Proficiency   B=Commendable
C=Satisfactory   D=Developing   E=Lacking

Skill Description   Your Rating

Skill Description	Your Rating
70. Motivate and lead people.	A B C D E
71. Organize people and tasks to achieve specific goals.	A B C D E
72. Assess a course of action in terms of its long-range effects.	A B C D E
73. Make decisions that will maximize both individual and collective good.	A B C D E
74. Appreciate the contributions of art, literature, science and technology to contemporary society.	A B C D E
75. Identify your own values.	A B C D E
76. Assess your values in relation to important life decisions.	A B C D E

A=Very High Proficiency   B=Commendable
C=Satisfactory   D=Developing   E=Lacking

EXERCISE 4
Grouping Your Transferable Skills

Before you began your self-assessment of the 76 skills in *Exercise 3* we noted that these individual skills can be grouped into nine categories. We recommended that you complete your assessment of the individual skills first. Now that you have analyzed each skill and assigned proficiency ratings to each, we suggest that you analyze them again grouped in the following nine categories:

Communication Skills (#1-8)

Research & Investigation Skills (#9-14)

Critical Thinking Skills (#15-23)

Personal & Career Development Skills (#24-37)

Information Management Skills (#38-43)

Human Relations & Interpersonal Skills (#44-56)

Design & Planning Skills (#57-65)

Management & Administrative Skills (#66-71)

Valuing Skills (#72-76)

These nine skill groups have all been identified repeatedly by employers and educators as areas of competence that are vital to success in many different life and career situations. As you examine the results of your skills assessment you may recognize some suggestive patterns of strengths and weaknesses in the nine categories. You may also notice that some skills are applicable in more than one category. There is nothing sacrosanct or permanent about these categories. You may wish to reorganize them or to create new ones that more closely fit your particular personality characteristics, your preferred learning style, and your specific learning objectives. You may notice for example, that we haven't specifically mentioned proficiency in computers. But, take a look at Skills 2, 4, 9, 13, 38, and 39 — all of which involve some aspect of communications or information management. It is very likely that a compilation of these computer-related skills will be important in almost any career you may choose, and will relate to other skill/career combinations as well.

Whether you are a student, a person engaged in a career search, an independent learner, or a little of each, you can assess and arrange past learning and design your future learning plan to highlight those areas of skill competence that are most important to your personal and professional needs.

Worksheet for Exercise 4: Grouping Your Transferable Skills

Instructions: 1. Record the quantity of "A's", "B's", etc. that you gave yourself in each of the nine categories from the Skills List.

2. Multiply each number you have recorded by the appropriate score (use a 4 for each "A", 3 for each "B", 2 for each "C", 1 for each "D", and 0 for each "E").

3. Total the five scores for each of the categories and divide each total by the actual number of skills in that category.

4. You may want to make a simple bar graph to display the results of your category ratings.

Sample Category Ratings
review before completing your own scoresheet

Communication
Skills (1-8)
  2 A's x 4 = 8
  3 B's x 3 = 9
  3 C's x 2 = 6
  0 D's x 1 = 0
  0 E's x 0 = 0

TOTAL   = 23
Divided by 8 = 2.87

Each of the calculations on the following pages will yield an average skill strength and indicate your relative competence in that particular skill category.

Your Own Category Ratings

Remember to make copies of these 2 pages to correspond to the number of Skills Lists you did. Also remember that the results are your personal and subjective ratings rather than an objective outside judgment of your qualifications for a particular career assignment.

Communication Skills (1-8)

____A's x 4 = ____·
____B's x 3 = ____·
____C's x 2 = ____·
____D's x 1 = ____·
____E's x 0 = ____·

TOTAL   = ____·
Divided by 8 = ____·

Critical Thinking Skills (15-23)

____A's x 4 = ____·
____B's x 3 = ____·
____C's x 2 = ____·
____D's x 1 = ____·
____E's x 0 = ____·

TOTAL   = ____·
Divided by 9 = ____·

Research & Investigation Skills (9-14)

____A's x 4 = ____·
____B's x 3 = ____·
____C's x 2 = ____·
____D's x 1 = ____·
____E's x 0 = ____·

TOTAL   = ____·
Divided by 6 = ____·

Personal & Career Development Skills (24-37)

____A's x 4 = ____·
____B's x 3 = ____·
____C's x 2 = ____·
____D's x 1 = ____·
____E's x 0 = ____·

TOTAL   = ____·
Divided by 14 = ____·

Information Management Skills (38-43)

___ A's x 4 = ___ •
___ B's x 3 = ___ •
___ C's x 2 = ___ •
___ D's x 1 = ___ •
___ E's x 0 = ___ •

TOTAL = ___ •
Divided by 6 = ___ •

Human Relations & Interpersonal Skills (44-56)

___ A's x 4 = ___ •
___ B's x 3 = ___ •
___ C's x 2 = ___ •
___ D's x 1 = ___ •
___ E's x 0 = ___ •

TOTAL = ___ •
Divided by 13 = ___ •

Design & Planning Skills (57-65)

___ A's x 4 = ___ •
___ B's x 3 = ___ •
___ C's x 2 = ___ •
___ D's x 1 = ___ •
___ E's x 0 = ___ •

TOTAL = ___ •
Divided by 9 = ___ •

Management & Administrative Skills (66-71)

___ A's x 4 = ___ •
___ B's x 3 = ___ •
___ C's x 2 = ___ •
___ D's x 1 = ___ •
___ E's x 0 = ___ •

TOTAL = ___ •
Divided by 6 = ___ •

Valuing Skills (72-76)

___ A's x 4 = ___ •
___ B's x 3 = ___ •
___ C's x 2 = ___ •
___ D's x 1 = ___ •
___ E's x 0 = ___ •

TOTAL = ___ •
Divided by 5 = ___ •

EXERCISE 5
Rating Your Transferable Skills

Having completed your skills assessment you now have a good profile of both your areas of skill strength and your areas of skill weakness. As suggested earlier, your areas of skill strength will be very helpful in exploring career fields as well as in writing resumes and in preparing for job interviews. Each of these activities is an essential part of the job search process and will be the subject of Exercises in *Task Five* later in this workbook.

Skills, Knowledge, Degrees:
What is Most Important for Success?

Experts differ in answering this question. As you look at your own categories of skills you may want to consider what one government official had to say about the career futures of children born in 1992 (the prospective high school graduating class of 2010): *"My advice to the class of 2010 would be the same as to the class of 1992: Make sure you have a broad range of verbal, analytic, math and science skills."*

The speaker was Ronald E. Kutscher, Associate Commissioner of the Labor Department's Bureau of Labor Statistics as quoted in *American*

Way, the in-flight magazine of American Airlines. (Jan. 15, 1992, pg. 156.) Mr. Kutscher suggested that *degrees* may not be as important as skills and knowledge: *"Our analyses indicate that at least through the year 2005, somewhere between twenty and thirty percent of those who get college degrees will end up working at a job that doesn't require that degree."*

So, what is the bottom line? According to the Associate Commissioner the key skill categories are those that contribute to *effective teamwork:* "... *social interaction becomes a key skill, as does the ability to organize teams of people, which often will be from different disciplines."*

Worksheet for Exercise 5:
The Skills Priority Grid

This Skills Priority Grid is an exercise designed to help you decide which of your skills it is important and possible to strengthen by further learning. It is important to remember that mastery of every skill is neither realistic or necessary for career success. Only those skills that are consistent with your values and personality, and those that are needed in your career should be considered for inclusion in your learning plan. The Skills Priority Grid will help you to place necessary and important skills in order.

You will notice that the Grid is divided into four quadrants. After you have identified your most important skill needs and plotted them on the Grid you will want to pay particular attention to the upper right quadrant. The skills that are placed in that quadrant are both of the highest importance, and in the most need of further learning. These will be likely prospects for further attention when you develop your learning plan in *Task 4* of this workbook.

Before you start on the worksheet it may help to review the Sample Grid on page 56. Ten skills are plotted on the grid. The horizontal scale represents the relative importance of the skill, while the vertical scale reflects the need for further learning. For example, the Sample Learner has rated "time management" (item "E") as having the highest importance by placing it in column #10 on the horizontal scale. But, on the vertical scale he has rated it as having little or no dependence on further learning by placing it at the bottom on line 1. The Sample Learner believes that he already has a high enough level of proficiency in time management. In contrast, he has rated "research" skills (item "G") as being very dependent on further learning by placing it in line 10 on the vertical scale. But he has placed it in column 5 on the horizontal scale because he doesn't consider it of the highest importance.

Sample Skills Priority Grid

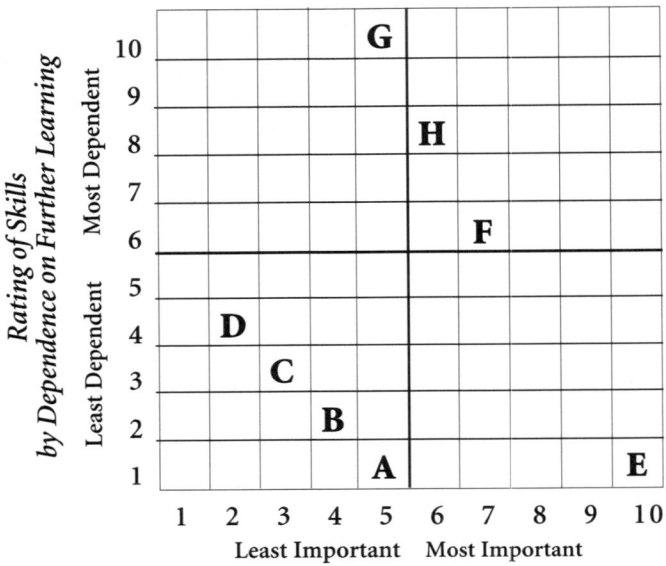

Sample List of Skills	Importance to You	Dependence on Further Learning
A. writing	5	1
B. critical thinking	4	2
C. supervision	3	3
D. organization	2	4
E. time management	10	1
F. planning	7	6
G. research	5	10
H. data processing	6	8

Instructions:

Step 1. Select the skills that are most important to your career success and enter them in the lettered spaces provided at the bottom of page 58. We recommend that you list a minimum of six.

Step 2. Rate each skill independently on a scale of 1 to 10 — "1" being the least important and "10" the most important. Enter that rating in the first column to the right of the listed skill.

Step 3. For each of these skills, estimate how much further learning you think you need to achieve the level of proficiency required for career success. Rate each on a scale of 1 to 10 — "1" indicates little learning required, a "10" indicates considerable learning required. Enter the rating in the second column to the right of the listed skill.

Step 4. Now plot each skill on your own Grid in the same way the sample skills are entered on the Sample Learner's Grid.

Your Skills Priority Grid

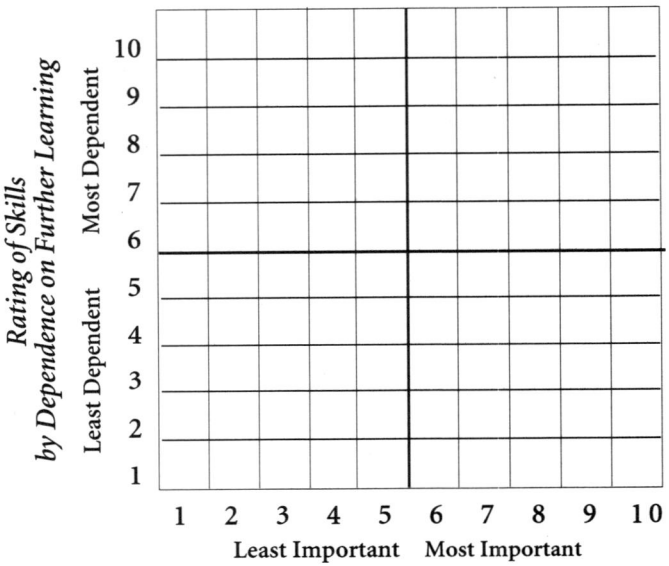

	Your List of Skills	Importance to You	Dependence on Further Learning
A.	_____		
B.	_____		
C.	_____		
D.	_____		
E.	_____		
F.	_____		
G.	_____		
H.	_____		

EXERCISES 6 and 7
Analyzing Your Skills in Action

You are nearly ready to match your values and skills to an appropriate career. Before you do, however, you need to test the strengths and the weaknesses of your skills profile against the realities of your everyday life.

We suggest that you take at least a week each for *Exercises 6 and 7* (strengths and weaknesses) to observe your performance in your job. If you aren't presently working you can substitute some other activity, such as "looking for a job". Work is the most useful environment for these exercises since the purpose is to improve your chances for career success. However, both exercises can be very helpful no matter what kind of activity you are engaged in during these two weeks.

There are several advantages to zeroing in on specific skills in specific work situations. As you observe your strengths you will be collecting important evidence for your resume and for use in job interviews. Analyzing specific applications of your strong skills will also help you to discover more

---

These exercises were developed from suggestions made by Professor John Dierke at San Francisco State University.

about how you acquired these skills. This will be helpful to you in *Task 4* when you develop your learning plans to improve some of your weaker skills.

As you observe your weaknesses you will have an excellent opportunity to begin developing your plans for bridging the gap between your present skills level and the levels required for career success. In some cases you may find weaker skills that you don't think you will be able to improve. If that appears to be the case, you might want to look ahead at our suggestions about dreaming as a vital part of the planning process (pg. 70) before you make a final decision. If you do conclude that there are some skills that you simply cannot develop, this knowledge will help you to avoid choosing a career in which you have little chance to succeed.

These two exercises will help you to get a clearer picture of your skills profile. The more you know about your strengths and weaknesses — and how they actually affect your performance in the workplace — the greater your chances are of finding the right match between you and a career. As you work on these exercises you may discover that one week is not enough. In fact you will probably find it helpful to develop a routine habit of observing and analyzing your strengths and weaknesses on the job. In *Exercise 16* we will suggest ways in which you can get the advantage of continuous feedback from your own evaluation of your work performance.

EXERCISE 6
Looking at Your Strong Skills in Action

Instructions: There are four parts to this exercise. Each one should be completed for each of the three skills you are analyzing.

Step 1. At the end of each day, review your performance, looking for an incident in which you successfully used one of your strong skills. When you settle on one that you think is important, write a brief paragraph describing the skill and the incident in which you used it successfully. Enter that information on the worksheet under Skill #1.

Step 2. Imagine that someone (perhaps a prospective employer) has asked you to prove that you possess this skill. Be prepared. Make a list of the evidence you think supports your conclusion that you successfully used this skill. For example, what good things happened as a result of your skill? Did anyone notice your performance and comment on it?

Step 3. Analyze the source of your strong skill. How did you develop this proficiency? Was it at school, or from studying a book, or listening to a lecture, or did you learn it experientially by "trial and error"? Or is there some other source, such as learning by example from your parents? The more you know about how you acquired your strong skills, the more success you will have in developing additional skills.

Step 4. Enter on your worksheet a preliminary plan for using this strength when you are asking for a job or for a promotion. How can this skill be reflected in your resume, or used in a job interview?

The worksheet has spaces for analyzing three different strong skills. We suggest that you do at least three during a week of self-observation and analysis. You may want to make extra copies of the worksheet so that you can analyze additional skills.

Worksheet for Exercise 6: Examining the Strengths in Your Transferable Skills Profile

	Skill #1
Step 1. Describe the skill and the specific situation in which you used it successfully.	
Step 2. Describe the evidence that confirms your conclusions. (e.g., successful outcome, or commendations).	

Step 3. How did you acquire this skill?
    education:
 	
    experience:
 	
    other:	

Step 4. How can this skill be used to add strength to your resume, and to your job interviews? (If this seems applicable, you may want to make notes now on pp. 129 and 139.)	

Skill #2	*Skill #3*

EXERCISE 7
Looking at Your Weaker Skills in Action

Instructions: This exercise has three steps. Each step should be completed for each of three weaknesses that you observe during the week.

Step 1. At the end of each day, review your performance looking for anything that you think you did not do well enough — or for anything that you did not even attempt to do because you were not confident of your ability to do it well enough. Write a brief paragraph on the worksheet describing the weak skill and the problem that resulted from it. What did you not do well, or not do at all because you doubted your ability to do it?

Step 2. Before you panic, ask yourself two questions about this instance of failure: a.) Is this particular weakness really important to your career success? (*i.e.,* Is your career success seriously threatened by your lack of strength in this skill area?) b.) Is this a weakness that it is possible for you to correct? Circle the appropriate "Yes" or "No" answers on the worksheet for each weakness.

Step 3. If you said "Yes" to both of these questions you have identified an important learning objective. Jot down your immediate thoughts about how you might plan to go about correcting this deficiency. (In *Task 4*, later in this workbook, you will be developing a more complete learning plan.) If you said "No" to the first question in Step 2 (Is this weakness an important factor in your success?) there is probably no need to do anything more. However, if you said "No" to the second question (Can you correct this weakness?) you will need to make sure that you choose a career in which this particular skill area is not needed for success.

The worksheet has space for analyzing three skill deficiencies. We suggest that you complete all three columns. You may wish to repeat the exercise if you find that it would be helpful to you in making a career choice (*Task 3*) or in developing a learning plan (*Task 4*).

Worksheet for Exercise 7: Examining the Weaknesses in Your Transferable Skills Profile

	Weakness #1
Step 1. Describe the skill that you needed and didn't have, and the problem that resulted from this weakness.	
Step 2. Is this a skill that: seems important? yes no is one that you think you are able to develop? yes no	
Step 3. If you answered yes to both of these questions, what *tentative** plans do you have for improving your skill level? **Note:* We said "tentative" because you will probably want to revise this plan after you complete *Task 4* later in the workbook.	

Weakness #2	Weakness #3
yes no	yes no
yes no	yes no

TASK THREE
Matching Your Profiles

Now that you have completed the development of your values and skills profiles you are in an excellent position to find the right match between you and your career. We suggest three steps in this process: *first*, take advantage of the resources available in libraries, bookstores, on the internet, and career centers; *second*, go into the field to conduct information interviews (*Exercise 8* on p. 74); and finally, test possible careers by doing internships.

Before you start this process, however, we think it is important for you to decide how high you want to set your career sights. There are two common mistakes that you will want to avoid: aiming too high; and aiming too low. If you aim for something that is impossible, you will invite a future of frustration and disappointment. If you aim too low you will always be a step or two below the career achievements that you deserve.

To find the right balance and achieve a perfect aim you need to make sure that the skills you assessed in *Task 2* are sufficient to achieve the values you have identified in *Task 1*. It is not as easy as it might seem. Your present skills level is not fixed. When you get to *Task 4* (bridging the gap) in this workbook you will be developing a contract with yourself to improve many of your skills and to achieve some new ones that you currently identify as weaknesses.

We believe that dreaming can play an important role in helping you to make the most effective career choice and to develop a realistic plan for success in that career. Success in the art of planning depends on finding the right relationship between what is desirable and what is possible. Where the planning process most often fails is in giving too much emphasis, too soon, to the question of possibility or impossibility. If we think first of what is possible, our tendency is to plan too low. We rule out too many things that may at first appear to be impossible, but are actually only difficult.

There is a reason why impossibility is hard to define. There are two kinds of impossibility: objective and subjective. For example, if you want to be President of the United States next year, and you are only 24 years old, it is actually impossible. The law of the land requires that Presidents be at least 35 years old — and it takes longer than a few months to change the Constitution. On the other hand, if you want to be President and you are already 35, but are a physically challenged woman who uses a wheelchair, you may be told that your dream is impossible—no woman has ever even been nominated for President—but the election of a physically challenged woman as President is only a *subjective* impossibility. There is no objective reason why it could not happen. Only a few decades ago it was thought to be impossible for a Catholic to become President, but then John F. Kennedy did. Not very many years ago it was said that a divorced person could not become President, but Ronald Reagan did. Social and educational progress make significant cultural growth and change possible.

For the art of planning to succeed we really need to start with dreaming. What do you really want as a career? After you have identified your true ultimate desire and then incorporated it into your learning plan, turn to the question of possibility. Be careful to distinguish between what may be *objectively* impossible and what is only *subjectively* "impossible".

The final step in successful planning is to choose a course of action somewhere in between the complete dream and your initial conclusions about what is possible. In other words, you should plan for at least a little bit more than you think is possible. Setting your sights high — but not to objectively impossible heights — will enhance your chances of career success. What it really comes down to is deciding how much extra effort you are willing to put into overcoming obstacles that seem at first glance to be impossible, but really just require a lot of determination and hard work.

Resources for Career Exploration

There are abundant resources to help you with choosing a career that fits your values and skills profiles. New print, audiovisual and computerized resources come onto the market regularly. Refer to the resources listed in the back of the book on pg. 146. There you will find suggestions for particular areas that you may want to research. Virtually all colleges and universities, and many high schools, have Career Centers with specialized libraries and computer programs to help with choosing a career. There are also many workshops, ranging from a few hours to as long as two weeks.

The value of the internet cannot be underestimated in your search for a career. Begin with the web addresses that we have provided and then see where your search takes you. One of the great joys of research is the process of connecting your particular interest with the related resources in the outside world, finding organizations, materials and people that can help you answer your questions and provide you with additional information. Using the internet, this process can give you immediate results, with nearly infinite links. The places your research can take you will help fuel your curiosity, spark ideas, and give you everything from hard data to personal anecdotes about careers that you are considering.

If you choose to utilize this vast resource, you will want to be aware that you can become easily mired down in volume. We would suggest beginning by browsing through the available information, and keeping a log of websites that interest you, or even a log of every one you have visited to avoid duplication in the future. Take notes on publications that are offered, or jot down ideas that come to you as you read. You will also be interested in searching and studying some of the websites under "Job Listings" or "Career Search" for informational purposes.

The distinction between "career" and "job" is not always evident in the media. Since the nature of work is constantly changing you can expect to find career information under various titles in newspaper, magazine and internet listings. There are frequent stories about emerging jobs and about the careers that are currently most accessible.

International Careers and Jobs

The Foreign Policy Association at www.fpa.org is a very good place for students and others to begin to explore their interest in an international career or job. There is also an excellent book in its fifth edition, called *International Jobs* by Eric Kocher and Nina Segal, that has been an authoritative guide for many years to launching and enhancing international careers. It provides substantial reference to pertinent websites and a wide range of career possibilities. (See Appendix on pg. 146 for more information.)

EXERCISE 8
Conducting Information Interviews

After you have started your review of available careers you will reach the point of departure for an exciting new process: interviewing people who are already established in one of the careers that you have decided might be just right for you.

Information interviews are different from job interviews. The information interview is only for the purpose of gathering information about a career. An information interview should provide you with two types of information: 1.) which values are, or are not, likely to be satisfied in a particular career; and 2.) what skills are needed for success in that career. Both of these types of information are vital to making an appropriate career choice. And the information you obtain about the skills needed for success will be very important in your selection of learning objectives to be included in your individualized learning plan (*Task 4*).

Suggestions for Conducting Information Interviews:

Step 1. In requesting an appointment, emphasize the fact that you are seeking *information*, not a job. This is very important because it puts the person you are interviewing in the respected position of an expert who can help you with information and opinions, rather than in the more stressful position of a potential employer who must evaluate you.

Step 2. Be prepared with questions that will give you information about career conditions that are related to your system of values.

Step 3. After the interview, translate the interviewee's responses into the terms of your own values. Your values and those of the interviewee may be quite different. For example, one of the things she may like most about her career is that it requires extensive travel. You, on the other hand, may have family or other values that are not compatible with extensive travel requirements.

Step 4. Finally, use the interview to obtain information about the skills and knowledge requirements that contribute to career success. Later, you can incorporate this information into your Learning Plan as essential learning objectives.

There is a strong possibility that there may be differences of opinion between you and your interviewee about the roles of various values and skills as ingredients of career success. It is a good idea to conduct several information interviews before making any final career or educational decisions. The internet will also yield substantial, relatively impartial information regarding a specific career area. Simply typing "careers in _____" and including your field of interest will provide you with many links to detailed information. It is also an excellent idea when you have completed your information gathering process, to discuss your conclusions with someone who knows you, and your values, very well.

Try not to be upset if the results of one or more information interviews seem to be negative. There may be a valuable message there, even if it isn't the one you hoped for. For example, you may go to an interview with high expectations about a particular career, and find that there are a lot of unexpected things you don't like about it. Of course, you may want to check out the validity of the results by interviewing another person in the same field. A second opinion is always a good idea. But you may well find out, even with several interviews, that the career you thought you would enjoy actually is not a very good match with your values and skills profiles. That may be disappointing, but it is a lot better than putting the time and effort into preparing for a career and then finding out, too late, that it is an unhappy choice. An information interview that seemed like a failure, in this case, really wasn't.

On the other hand, you also need to be careful about initial interviews that seem to confirm your hopes about a career. What seems like a positive reinforcement could be in error if the person you interviewed has very different values from yours. She may feel very positive about a career environment that you would not find compatible with your own values. Again, a second opinion is a good idea. It may confirm your positive impressions, or it may uncover some important additional questions for you to consider.

How many information interviews should you undertake? Sometimes just two or three will give a sufficiently clear view of the match with your values and skills profiles. And sometimes it may take many interviews before you feel ready to make a final career decision.

Fortunately, it is easy to develop an information interview habit. In addition to formally scheduled interviews you can add to your valuable store of information many times simply by being ready to take advantage of casual opportunities that may arise. Anytime you meet someone who is, or once was, in a career field you are considering, be ready to explore informally the ways in which your values and skills profiles may fit, or may not fit, into any prospective career environments. This kind of observation and research will make a worthwhile addition to your Lifelong Learning Journal.

Worksheet for Exercise 8: Information Interviews

Instructions: After each interview fill out a copy of the data sheets on the following pages. There are at least five kinds of information to cover: values; skills; employment opportunities; salary and benefits; special qualifications such as degrees, licenses, age, citizenship, etc. There is also space for additional notes you may want to make (*e.g.*, suggestions for other contacts). Room is left after the first item for you to "translate" the interviewee's comments about values into your own values preferences.

Information Interview Data Sheet
you may want to make extra copies of this sheet

Date _____

Person Interviewed _____

Company/Business _____

Your Career/Job Interest _____

_____

_____

1. Person's values met or not met _____

_____

_____

_____

Your own values preferences are in agreement or not

_____

_____

_____

_____

_____

Things the person likes about this career

_____

_____

_____

_____

_____

_____

Things the person dislikes about this career

_____
_____
_____
_____

2. Skills and knowledge needed for career success

_____
_____
_____
_____
_____

3. Employment prospects _____

_____
_____

4. Salary and benefits _____

5. Other qualifications _____

_____
_____

Notes _____

_____
_____
_____

Conclusions

The Task you have just completed, *Matching Your Profiles,* is probably not complete for all time. "Change" is the most permanent characteristic of employment in our contemporary culture. New kinds of jobs and careers emerge continuously. One expert has estimated that as many as 4 out of 5 jobs that exist in any one year will not exist 5 years later. And change happens to people, too. Both your values and your skills will change from year to year. As a result of both of these kinds of changes, those to you and those to the economic environment, some experts estimate that you may have as many as 5 to 7 careers in your lifetime. Even allowing for the hazy line between "job" and "career" this means that you can anticipate returning to *Task 3* — perhaps several times — as your career progresses.

Matching you to your work is a recurring activity. The only way to make sure that you are happy and successful in your career is to keep your options open. As you change, and as the nature of the working world changes, you will always need to be ready to make adjustments. Rather than waiting for a crisis, the best idea is to schedule periodic reviews of your career status. Mark your calendar for an annual evaluation of the continuing match between your personal profiles and your career commitments.

TASK FOUR
Bridging the Gap

You have now completed the first three vital steps toward career success:

- Your values profile is an accurate reflection of what you want in a career.
- Your skills profile is an accurate picture of your strengths and weaknesses.
- Your exploration of possible careers has given you a preliminary picture of the skills gap between the strengths you already have and those you must improve in order to succeed.

Now you are ready for the next step: a learning plan to bridge the gap between where you are and where you want to go. A learning plan should tell you how to improve your skill levels from where they are to where you want them to be.

But first, a reminder: bear in mind that the results of the first three steps are subject to change. Your values may shift, your skills profile will continue to improve, and — most importantly — your career preferences may change. In a very important sense all five steps in your career success plan are always open to review and revision. Career success requires continued effort to maintain an effective match between you and your work.

Because of this constant change, bridging the gap between the present and career success is a continuous process. A good way to focus the meaning of this fact is to look back at Skill #24 in *Exercise 3*, and to elevate it to the status of a Master Skill: *learning how to learn*. Career success depends on this skill more than on any other. If you develop a high level of learning proficiency you will always be one huge step ahead of the crowd. Nothing is more important to continued career success than learning how to learn.

What is Your Learning Style?

Because your learning efficiency level is so vitally important, the first step toward bridging the gap is to determine your personal learning style. People learn in different ways. There are two basic types of learning — traditional and experiential — and many combinations in between:

1. Some of us prefer to learn from reading books,

listening to lectures and participating in formal activities directed by a teacher or instructor. This is usually called traditional or classroom learning.

2. Others of us prefer to learn from *doing* something, practicing and experimenting on our own. This is called experiential learning.

Of course, all of us learn in both ways. What will be most useful to you is to find the right combination, for you, of traditional and experiential learning. If you know what kind of learner you are, and if you assume full and active responsibility for directing your own learning process, you will greatly magnify your chances for career success.

The Learning Style Inventory

As a starting place to defining your own learning style, we recommend that you complete the *Kolb Learning Style Inventory* (LSI3, updated 1999). The LSI3 measures an individual's strengths and weaknesses as a learner. The Inventory can be completed online or on paper.[*] Although David Kolb's work is often referred to as a theory of experiential learning it applies as well to traditional learning. As you see in the diagram on the following page, Kolb identifies four steps in the learning process: concrete experience, reflective observation, abstract conceptuali-

---

[*]For a very good informational site and to locate a source for the Inventory, visit www.hayresourcesdirect.haygroup.com or contact Hay Resources Direct, 116 Huntington Avenue, Boston MA 02116, 800-729-8074.

zation, and active experimentation. The concrete experience can be a "passive" experience such as reading a book or listening to a lecture. Or it can be an "active" experience such as building a house or managing a campaign.

What Kolb's LSI3 does is to measure your personal preferences for each of the four defined parts of the learning process. Then your four scores are combined by a mathematical formula to describe what kind of learner you are.

The KOLB Learning Cycle

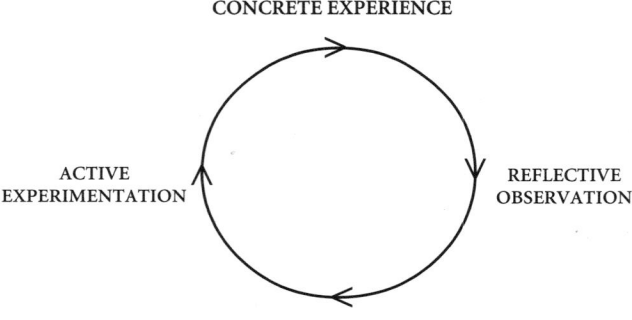

Whether you choose the Kolb LSI3 or some other exercises to determine your learning style, the most important thing is for you to know what your style is. After you know what kind of learner you are you may wish to work on making some adjustments. For example, if you find that you are near one end of the scale — either very much a traditional learner, or very much an experiential learner — you may want to consider the development of some additional learning strengths.

Enhancing your learning style would be sure to address reservations often expressed by employers about both the very traditional learner and the very experiential learner. The complaint about the traditional learner (strong in reflective observation and abstract conceptualization) is that, although they may know a lot about theory, they are not so effective when it comes to applying the theory in real life situations. On the other hand, the complaint about experiential learners (strong in active experimentation and concrete experience) is that, although they may be effective in doing something in one particular setting, they may not perform as well in unfamiliar settings because they don't know the theoretical explanations for what they are doing.

In summary, what you need to do is: define your style; find the right balance, for you, of traditional and experiential learning methods; and then make any adjustments that seem both necessary and possible to develop the most effective learning style you can.

Most of us have been trained to believe that learning and education are the same and that they come primarily, if not exclusively, from going to school. It's simply not true. Take a look at the differences between education and learning in your own life. You are a student for only a few years, but a learner for a lifetime. And, for most of us, that transition from student to self-directed learner underlines the importance of developing a learning style that is appropriately balanced between traditional and experiential learning.

The Elements of a Good Learning Plan

Once you have identified your learning style (and considered any necessary adjustments) you can develop an effective learning plan to bridge the gap between the skills you have and the skills you need for career success.

A good learning plan has three parts:

1.) identifying learning objectives;

2.) developing learning activities to achieve those objectives; and

3.) monitoring your progress through periodic evaluation.

Now *Exercise 9: Identifying Your Learning Needs, Exercise 10: Selecting Your Learning Activities and Resources*, and *Exercise 11: Evaluating Your Progress*, will help you address each of these three sections in turn. When you have finished this process you will be prepared to complete your own comprehensive learning plan.

EXERCISE 9
Identifying Your Learning Needs

How can you decide which learning objectives are most important to your career success? One way is to review *Exercise 5* (your Skills Grid on page 58). In that exercise you identified your most important skill needs and put them in priority order; then you rated them in the order of their dependence on further learning. Those skills that landed in the upper right quadrant are likely candidates for important learning needs. Before entering these skills on your Learning Needs Grid, you may want to consider the following suggestions.

You completed *Exercise 5* before you identified any specific career. It was an inventory of your career-transferable skills. In the meantime you have completed *Task 3: Matching Your Profiles.* Now you may want to make some changes in the worksheet from *Exercise 5* as you think of the importance of each skill with reference to a particular career. For example, you may have placed some information management skills on the grid, but judged them to be only 6th or 7th in terms of their importance and dependence on further learning. Now, however, you may have discovered that you are interested in becoming a member of a television news team, or some other career environment in which information management is of overriding importance. Perhaps you will want to shift information management to a higher category. And there may be some skills in the original exercise that you gave higher priority, but can now be lowered in view of the specific career(s) you are considering.

> ### Suggestion about International Careers
>
> When you completed *Exercise 5* you were working with career-*transferable* skills. Remember that we alerted you that once you have chosen a line of work you will then have both career-specific and job-specific skills to consider in addition to the career-transferable skills listed in *Exercise 5*. For example, if *Task 3* has led you to a career in the export-import field with an emphasis on the Orient, you may now want to consider adding some vitally important language skills to your Grid. Learning Japanese or Chinese may now become one of your most important learning objectives. Review other cultural learning skills that you may need to apply to your chosen international career and see where you may need to make further adjustments, possibly adding additional necessary skills to your Learning Plan.

Before you complete your Learning Needs Grid: take another look at your Values Grid, *Exercise 2*, pg. 29, as well. When you completed that Exercise you made an estimate about the additional learning needed to ensure that each value would be most likely to be satisfied. Look at the Values Grid again, particularly in the upper right quadrant. Given your career decision, or progress toward one, in *Task 3*, are there new, more specific reasons to identify certain learning needs related to maximizing your chances for values satisfaction?

Considering the above suggestions, review your original Skills Priority Grid and make any revisions and/or additions that you consider appropriate. It is especially important to pay close attention to the prioritizing of these needed skills because, once you have completed your Learning Needs Grid, you will be translating the most critical needs into learning objectives in preparation for *Exercise 10: Selecting Your Learning Activities and Resources*. A little extra thought now will ensure that the time you spend pursuing new learning activities will have the most positive and immediate results possible.

You will now use this revised list of important skills to complete the Learning Needs Grid and the List of Learning Objectives on the next three pages.

Worksheet for Exercise 9: Your Learning Needs Grid and List of Learning Objectives

Instructions:

Step 1: Transfer the skills from your revised Skills Priority Grid to your list of needs below the grid on the next page. Transfer the adjusted rankings of importance and dependence on learning for those skills to the columns to the right of the list.

Step 2: Enter those skills on the Learning Needs Grid according to the new rankings.

Step 3: When you have completed your grid, take a closer look at the needs that are entered in the upper right hand quadrant. These are both important and highly dependent on further learning. Restate each of these needs as a learning objective on the list on page 92. For example, if the skill "data processing" is identified as an important skill that is dependent on further learning, you could restate that as a learning objective by entering "improve data processing skills" or "learn more about computers" on your List of Learning Objectives. List your objectives in priority order, beginning with the most important. This will be the skill that falls closest to the upper right hand corner of the grid — the one with the highest combined ranking for importance and dependence on learning.

Your Learning Needs Grid

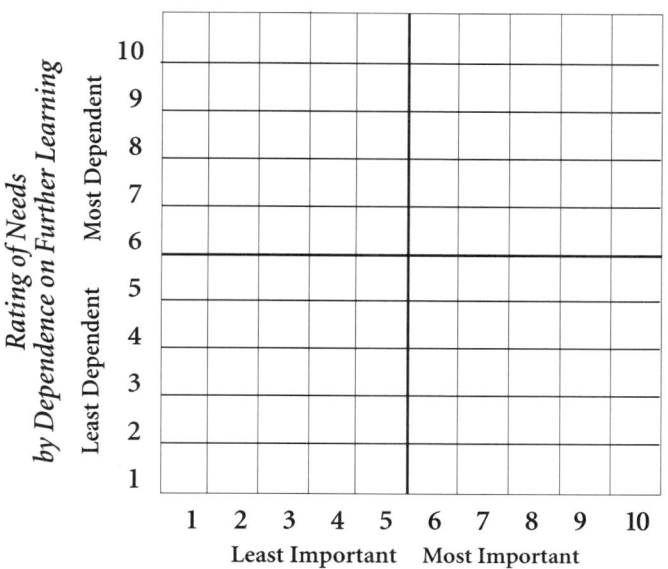

	Your List of Needs	Importance to You	Dependence on Further Learning
A.	_____		
B.	_____		
C.	_____		
D.	_____		
E.	_____		
F.	_____		
G.	_____		
H.	_____		

List of Learning Objectives

1. _____
   _____

2. _____
   _____

3. _____
   _____

4. _____
   _____

5. _____
   _____

6. _____
   _____

You should probably treat this as a "living" list. New learning objectives will emerge and priorities will change. And, of course, the happiest result will be when you can cross off those objectives that you have achieved.

As you approach the next part of your Learning Plan (selecting activities and resources) it will probably be best to work on one objective at a time. While you may actually be learning several things at any given time, it is important to plan the learning activities separately for each learning objective. At the end of this Task, on page 105, you will find a Learning Plan Summary. You may want to make more copies as your career development progresses.

EXERCISE 10
Selecting Your Learning Activities and Resources

Now that you have identified your learning objectives and put them in priority order, the next step is to select appropriate learning activities and resources to help you achieve those objectives.

Later, as you develop your Learning Plans you will need to choose different combinations of activities and resources appropriate to each learning objective. First, however, it will be helpful to develop two general lists: *Learning Activities* that are compatible with your learning style; and *Learning Resources* — people, places and things — that are available to help you. You will be able to draw on this pool of activities and resources as you develop various specific learning plans for each of your objectives.

As you complete Worksheet 10.1 remember that you will want to have balanced learning plans that combine theory and practice by using both traditional learning and experiential learning activities.

As you complete the related Worksheet 10.2 you will strengthen your future learning plans by considering all of the people, places and things available to help with your learning.

Worksheet for Exercise 10.1: Learning Activities

Instructions: Remember that this is a general list — a pool of potential activities from which you will later select those that are appropriate to your various learning needs. As you complete this list take another look at the learning objectives you have listed in *Exercise 9*. Include here *all* of the Learning Activities that might be helpful in addressing those needs.

Among the more traditional learning activities you may want to include on your list are: school and college courses, lectures, and reading. Among the experiential learning activities you might want to consider are: projects at your work, volunteer activities, consultation with experts and independent study and research.

Traditional Learning Activities To Help You Achieve Your Goals
courses, tutors, lectures, reading, etc.

_____

_____

_____

_____

_____

_____

_____

_____

Experiential Learning Activities
To Help You Achieve Your Goals
paid/volunteer work, projects, individual study/practice, etc.

Worksheet for Exercise 10.2: Learning Resources

Instructions: This is just a general list of all the resources that you might want to consider when preparing learning plans for each of your specific objectives. As you complete this list it will help to take another look at your worksheets for *Exercises 9* and *10.1*. This list should include all of the people, places and things that might help you to complete the activities on Worksheet 10.1 and achieve the objectives you listed in *Exercise 9*.

Among the *people* resources you may want to think about are: family and friends, your employers and other work colleagues, and experts in various fields. Among the *places* you might consider are: libraries, your work environment, and the sites of any volunteer or recreational activities where there are experiential learning opportunities. Among the *things* you could have on your resource list are: radio and television programs, audio, video and computer products, printed materials and the internet.

People *who can help you achieve your career goals*

_____
_____
_____
_____
_____
_____

_____
_____
_____
_____
_____

Places that can help you achieve your career goals

_____
_____
_____
_____
_____
_____
_____
_____

Things that can help you achieve your career goals

_____
_____
_____
_____
_____
_____
_____

EXERCISE 11
Evaluating Your Progress

Continuous evaluation of your learning progress is the third and final element in a good learning plan. In this Exercise you are asked to list the people who can help you to evaluate your progress. In addition you may want to list any testing instruments that may be available for measuring your proficiency levels in the skill and knowledge areas covered in your learning plans.

Evaluation can tell you two things: what level of proficiency you have reached; and how effective your learning plan is (*e.g.*, whether you are progressing as far, or as fast, as you could). Determining your level of proficiency is called *summative* evaluation. It answers the question: How much progress have you made? It is the result of this kind of summative evaluation that you will want to reflect on your resume and in your job interviews.

Formative evaluation is the name usually given to the process of determining how effective your learning plan is. It is this kind of evaluation that we are most concerned with in this Exercise. Of course, the first step in making an accurate formative evaluation is a summative evaluation: what kind of proficiency have you reached? But it is vital to your career success to go an important step further and determine how effective your learning plan is. Are you achieving your objective as rapidly and effectively as possible? Are the learning activities you have chosen and the resources you are using doing the best job for you? In *Exercise 11* you are asked to identify the resources — both people and testing instruments — that can help you to answer these questions.

Self-Evaluation

The first evaluation resource is yourself. There are two advantages to self-evaluation: *first*, you know yourself and your circumstances better that anyone else does; and, *second*, you are the one with the strongest interest in your success. You have already had one exposure to self-evaluation — *Exercise 3*, in which you judged your proficiency in each of 76 career-transferable skills. You will have another self-evaluation opportunity in *Exercise 16: The Lifelong Learning Log*.

Along with the advantages of knowing yourself and having the greatest stake in the outcome, there are also two potential disadvantages: subjectivity and lack of expertise. It is difficult to be objective enough to get a really accurate assessment by self-evaluation. Sometimes you may overrate yourself and sometimes you may underrate yourself. In addition, since you are trying to expand your knowledge and skill you are necessarily dealing with subject matter that is not completely familiar to you. To guard against these two potential problems — subjectivity and the fact that you are a learner rather than an expert — it is important to identify some sources of help. What you want to add to your self-evaluation is objectivity and expertise.

In this Exercise you are asked to list two kinds of help: people who may be able to assist you with the evaluation of your learning progress; and any testing instruments that may be available for use in measuring your level of proficiency. For traditional learning activities there are often some built-in evaluators. If you are taking a course, for example, the instructor usually provides both formative and summative evaluation in the form of progress reports, grades or conferences. Many books and computerized learning resources have objective examinations included as part of the learning package.

With experiential learning you are more likely to be on your own to evaluate your progress. It is always important to involve as many people as possible in your evaluation. Friends and family members, even if they are not particularly expert in the subject matter, can be very helpful in avoiding the subjectivity problems of over and underrating yourself. Subject matter experts may be available, with varying degrees of expertise, from various sources. Often the most helpful sources of expertise are in your workplace. Among the best potential sources of evaluation are your supervisor and co-workers who may have both personal and professional interests in your progress, as well as significant expertise in the subject you are studying.

As you work on *Exercise 11* it will be helpful to review the lists of resources you made on Worksheet 10.2. Some of the same people you identified as helpful learning resources may be equally helpful in monitoring your progress and evaluating the results.

Worksheet for Exercise 11: Evaluating Your Progress

The evaluation component of your Learning Plan will evolve as your learning progresses. Some elements of it depend on the specific characteristics of your learning objectives and activities. However, there are some things that should be in place from the beginning. As you did in *Exercises 10.1* and *10.2*, you can develop on this Worksheet some of the more general resources from which you can make your specific evaluation plans for each learning objective.

Instructions: While the specifics will vary with each learning objective, it is important to mark your calendar with regular reminders about evaluation. Under this item you may want to identify an annual date (or perhaps semi-annual or even quarterly) on which you will review your evaluation needs. (*Suggestion:* It might be helpful to choose a special date like the one sometimes referred to as the "half-birthday" — on the opposite side of the calendar, six months from your real birthday.)

Evaluation Timetable
regular dates for considering evaluation needs

_____
_____
_____
_____
_____
_____

People Who Can Help
evaluate your progress

_____
_____
_____
_____
_____
_____
_____
_____

Testing Instruments
to evaluate your progress

_____
_____
_____
_____
_____
_____

EXERCISE 12
Completing Your Learning Plans

You are now ready to bridge the gap between where you are and where you want to be. You have previewed all three essential parts of a successful learning plan:

- in *Exercise 9:* you identified learning needs and objectives,

- in *Exercises 10.1* and *10.2:* you selected learning activities and the resources to support them,

- in *Exercise 11:* you evaluated your learning progress,

and in *Exercise 12* you will be combining these three components into a complete learning plan.

Before you fill in the Worksheet on the next page we recommend that you make several copies. You will need one for each separate learning objective you want to achieve. It is a good idea to preserve a master copy in your files. Learning is a lifelong — and career-long — process. The effort you put into effective learning will pay major dividends in future career success.

Worksheet for Exercise 12:
Learning Plan Summary
Combining Exercises 9, 10 & 11

This is your Learning Plan for bridging the gap between the skills and knowledge you have and the skills and knowledge you will likely need for career success. This Plan will also be a good ongoing list to keep in your career journal. It will serve as a commitment to the recognition of lifelong learning throughout your career.

Instructions:

1. Use one worksheet for *each* of the learning objectives from *Exercise 9* (p. 92).

2. On the worksheet, enter the learning activities that are appropriate for this particular learning objective. List the people and other resources that you will utilize as you undertake the learning activities described for this plan.

3. Describe the evaluation process you will use, listing the people who can help and any evaluation instruments or measurements such as tests or performance examinations.

Your Personal Learning Plan
make several copies, one for each objective

Learning Objective

_____
_____
_____
_____
_____
_____

Learning Activities to Achieve Objectives

Traditional	Experiential
_____	_____
_____	_____
_____	_____
_____	_____
_____	_____
_____	_____
_____	_____
_____	_____
_____	_____
_____	_____

Learning Resources to Achieve Objective

People   **Places & Things**

_____   _____
_____   _____
_____   _____
_____   _____
_____   _____
_____   _____
_____   _____
_____   _____

Evaluation Processes to Achieve Objective

People   **Tests, etc.**

_____   _____
_____   _____
_____   _____
_____   _____
_____   _____
_____   _____
_____   _____
_____   _____

TASK FIVE
Sharpening Your Skills

At the beginning of this workbook we urged you to consider the differences between "careers" and "jobs." While it is most important for you to have your own personal definition, we also suggested that you make room in that definition for the following:

Career emphasizes the kind of work you are doing over a long period of time;

Job refers to the more immediate, short range status of where and for whom you are working.

Given those basic differences between careers and jobs, you can safely conclude that long term career success depends on being able to get and hold the right jobs at the right times. In the first four tasks in this workbook you have been working primarily on *career* questions: What kind of work activity do you like? What kinds of things do you do well? What careers match those values and skills? How and what do you need to learn in order to ensure your career success?

While the answers to those questions may not be cast in stone, you can now turn to the process of weaving your current answers to those four questions into a complete and effective success package.

How do you do it? What are "job-seeking skills" and where do you get them?

The standard answers to those questions are: writing a good resume; and conducting successful job interviews. We will get to both of these important skills a little later, but in addition to these skills there are also some less tangible factors that may play a role in getting a job. It is accurate to describe them as "wild cards."

Heredity, Luck and Influence: Three Wild Cards

Let's start with these three "wild cards"—things that you don't find in most job-seeking formulas, but that are, nevertheless, often vitally important in determining the success of your job search.

Wild Card #1:   First, there is a simple, but powerful fact: the kind of person you are. What do you look like? How old are you? What is your personality? Skin color? Gender? We can't deny that some or all of these things may make a difference when you are looking for a job. Laws can be passed against discrimination, but if an employer has preferences based on age, gender, or ethnic origin, these preferences can, and often do, make a difference—especially when there is a large pool of more or less equally qualified applicants. Personal characteristics such as these may tip the scales in either direction— for you or against you.

In any case, a range of personal characteristics may be the source of hidden disadvantages, or advantages, in the job-seeking process. Some experts suggest that an interviewer may sometimes make a final decision about you in the first ten seconds of the interview—even before you say anything.

While there is no magic way to eliminate this particular "wild card" it is important to be aware of it. It is helpful to have a good idea of the assets you start with and to know where you may have to perform especially well in order to qualify for a job. In the rest of this chapter— including our discussion of the other two wild cards—there is ample room for manipulating the whole deck of cards. You can play them up or play them down.

Wild Card #2: Many job successes just happen. You may be at the right place at the right time. For example, the phone may ring with good news just before you were going out the door. (Or, of course, it may not ring until you are already gone—and have forgotten to turn on the answering machine.) Being at the right place at the right time, or meeting the right person in the right circumstances may be pure luck. Being vigilant about your career objective and placing it high on your priority list can also increase your chances of getting "lucky."

Also, the more you do to make yourself available at that "right place" or to that "right person" the more likely the luck is to happen. In a word, another way to maximize your luck is *networking*. You will hear the discouraging news that "most jobs aren't gotten through excellent resumes or scintillating interview performances, but by other "connections" (such as those that come by pure luck, or as in the case of the next wild card, by having influence).

You can multiply your "connections" by putting a lot of attention to networking. Tell a lot of people that you are looking for a job. Make it a part of your daily conversational habit. Convert your job search into a campaign, letting as many people as possible know what you are seeking.

Wild Card #3: "Influence" is generally viewed as something improper, but nevertheless often very effective. For example: "The boss's daughter got the job because . . .". On the other hand, the acceptable practice of giving *references* is also a way of focusing some helpful, and legitimate, influences for your prospective employer to consider. The most cynical comment you may hear about job seeking is that, "it's not *what* you know, but *who* you know that gets you the job." Of course that is not always the case. Yet it often does make a difference who is on your side when a hiring decision is made.

Resumes and Job Interviews

These are the two traditional pillars of job-seeking skill. It is said, "A good resume will get you the interview," and "a good interview will get you the job." As we have already seen, this isn't always true and certainly isn't the only way in which jobs are secured. We cannot overemphasize however, that the job seeker needs to have a current resume and needs to be an accomplished interviewee.

In *Exercises 14* and *15* we will work on both of these tasks. We will review some of the "rules" for resumes and interviews. More to the point, we will help you to develop your own response to the continuing stream of advice, good and bad, that appears in books and articles about resumes and the interview process.

Actually, there are only two undeniable and basic rules about resumes and job interviews:

1. know yourself; and

2. know as much as you can about the person (or persons) who will read your resume and who will interview you.

We will talk more about this second rule later when we get to *Exercise 14: Writing Your Resume* and *Exercise 15: Preparing for Your Job Interviews.*

First, let's take a closer look at Rule #1, know yourself. Virtually all of the experts about resumes and interviews cite this as a cardinal rule. You have already begun to work on it: your values and skills profiles are essential to successful job seeking. You will want to review both of them again before you write your resume or develop your interviewing strategy. *Exercise 13* which follows will not only help you with a review of your values and skills, but will summarize a more complete collection of all your career-relevant experience.*

---

*As his doctoral project (Union Institute, Cincinnati, 1997) Dr. Larry Linden developed the concept of a "holistic career portfolio" that included the relevant personal as well as professional strengths of the individual. He argues that, "It is the whole person who is hired for a job, not just the skill set that is required–thus the language *holistic* portfolio."

EXERCISE 13
Creating Your Career Relevance Profile

There are two checklists to be completed in this exercise. The first covers your formal learning from traditional schools and colleges; the second details your experience and learning from all other sources such as work, volunteer activities, recreation and leisure, and your personal life.

Checklist #1: Before you complete this checklist you should review your educational records. (If you don't already have a file marked "education" it's a good time to make one.) Get out your diplomas, certificates, degrees and transcripts. Some of the evidence you will want to include in your comprehensive career relevance profile is obvious: certification from schools and colleges that you have completed various courses of study. But there is important additional evidence that you will need to think about. For example, if you are a college graduate you will have on your record a "major." That is important to potential employers because it certifies that you have a "depth component" or specialization in your education. But it can be misleading and it doesn't tell the whole story. In most cases a major is only a little more than a fourth of the total degree program. You need to be prepared to tell the rest of the story. What did you learn in the other 70% or so of your studies? Was there a theme, or cluster of courses, a project, some area of concentration that you yourself built into your education, but that doesn't show as a major, or even as a minor, on your official transcript?

If your major was International Relations or one of the Social Sciences or Humanities, you should be prepared to show that you also concentrated some of your electives in business, or data processing, or some other relevant area that has given you a breadth of educational preparation appropriate for an international career. If your major was in Business you will want to be prepared to describe the liberal arts studies you have completed. Employers usually prefer to hire people with a good balance between liberal studies and professional studies.

A good general education includes: problem solving, critical thinking, communication skills and learning how to learn.

Sometimes a "MAJOR" seems to get pasted like an exclusive label across the forehead of a job applicant. You are the primary source of correction to this common assumption of your educational background and experience.

While most high school transcripts do not list a major, you may have had a special interest at that level of education too. Review everything. It is up to you to convert the meager, sometimes misleading messages of high school and college certification into accurate and meaningful reflections of what you have really learned in your formal education.

Checklist #2: The second checklist extends your career relevance profile in two ways. It adds new dimensions to the record of your learning, and it also documents your career-relevant experience. Learning (both knowledge and skills) and experience are both important to prospective employers. They are interested in what you know, what you can do, and how much experience you have had in applying your knowledge and skills.

As you fill in the second checklist it may be helpful to write a brief autobiography. Go back over your entire life, looking at every year carefully, to rediscover each of the life experience that may have contributed to the development of the experiential qualities an employer is seeking.

Suggestion for Adult Learners

If you haven't finished college, and if you have significant non-collegiate learning experience, here is a tip: Checklist 13.2 may have very special meaning for you. Many colleges and universities have adult learning programs. Many of these programs offer credit for college-level learning acquired from work and other experience. It isn't "giveaway" credit. It is credit for learning, not for experience *per se.* It takes some significant effort on your part to document and present it for evaluation. It must meet quality assurance standards. But if you think that your completed Checklist 13.2 reflects creditable college-level learning, it may be worthwhile for you to take a look at Lois Lamdin's book *Earn College Credit for What You Know*. (See reference in *Appendix* pg. 149 for more information on this excellent book.)

As with several other exercises in this workbook you will find it very helpful to discuss this exercise with people who know you and your personal history well. Some of the relevant experiences in your life may be so much a part of you that you don't notice them as sources of career-relevant strengths. You will maximize the value of your career-relevance profile* by discussing it thoroughly with people who know you well.

In addition to the two checklists you may want to make a list of other items such as: letters of recommendation, commendations, awards, newspaper clippings about your activities and accomplishments, photographs, and other documentation of career-relevant experience.

---

*The idea of a "career-relevance profile" was developed from suggestions made by Dr. Donald Casella at San Francisco State University.

Worksheet for Exercise 13.1: Checklist #1 Traditional Learning

Instructions: This is a record of your formal learning in schools, colleges, seminars and workshops. Your diplomas, degrees and other certificates of completed coursework should be listed here.

High School   Name _____

Diploma _____ Date _____

Other certificates or honors _____

_____

_____

_____

Areas of concentration _____

_____

_____

_____

_____

College/University   Name _____

make copies of this worksheet to list more than one institution

Degrees and Dates _____

_____

_____

_____

_____

_____

Major Areas of Study _____

_____
_____
_____

Minors/Special Study _____

_____
_____
_____

General Education _____

_____
_____

Field-based Learning *(internships, cooperative education, study abroad and community service learning)*

_____
_____
_____
_____
_____

Other Formal Learning *(for which you have transcripts or other certification: weekend and evening courses, special seminars, on-the-job training, military service courses, etc.)*

_____
_____
_____
_____
_____
_____

Worksheet for Exercise 13.2: Checklist #2 Untranscripted Experiential Learning

Instructions: This is just a checklist of possible sources of experiential learning that may provide important information for your resume and job interviews. As you are reminded of important things you have learned from experience you should make a brief note on this worksheet. Later, as you work on your resume and plan for your job interviews, review this worksheet and make additional notes as necessary to describe the learning outcomes you wish to highlight for your prospective employers.

Learning at Work Paid Employment _____

_____
_____
_____

Volunteer Jobs _____

_____
_____
_____

International and Intercultural Activities

Travel _____

_____
_____

Residence Abroad _____

_____

Leisure Activities, Hobbies   Creative Arts *(painting, writing, music, dancing, crafts, etc.)* _____

_____

_____

Reading, Independent Study _____

_____

Recreation _____

Other _____

Organizational Activities   Leadership _____

_____

_____

Committee Work _____

Public Speaking _____

Fundraising _____

Other _____

_____

Family and Other Personal Activities

Marriage _____ Children _____

Money Management _____

Organization and Planning _____

_____

Construction and Repairs _____

Nutrition _____

Relocation _____ Illness _____

Death _____ Divorce _____

EXERCISE 14
Writing Your Resume

Instructions: You have already completed the major steps in preparation for writing your resume: your values and skills profiles; your efforts to match those profiles to appropriate careers; and the comprehensive career relevance profile that you just completed in *Exercise 13*. You are almost ready to write the first draft of your resume (or to review and update your old resume).

First, however, you will have to make decisions about two vital aspects of this important document: its *content* — what you are going to put in it; and its *form* — how you will organize and print it. Then, after you finish your resume you will need to make some decisions about how to use it: how to present it, including the possibility of a good cover letter, and to whom.

Cover Letters and Resumes: One Employer's Attitudes

As with everything else about resumes, it should come as no surprise to you that there are many different ideas about cover letters.

Example: An article written by an employer in New York City tells about the way she responded to more than 600 letters with resumes that she received in the mail in response to her advertisement. First, she threw out, without opening them, all that abbreviated New York City as "N.Y.C." on the envelope. After opening the remainder she tossed out, without reading them, all that began: "To Whom It May Concern" (although she hadn't bothered to give them her name). After applying still more of her "rules" ("quaint personal preferences," some might say) she finally read only a handful of resumes — choosing only those that began with "Dear Heart" or "Dear Gentleperson."

The moral of this true story is this: remember that there are no universally accepted rules about resumes, only personal preferences. And these are sure to vary widely.

On both content and form there are literally hundreds of books and articles that are full of "rules" for you to follow about resumes. These rules often contradict each other. One expert says that the most important thing is to include a description of your skills; another says that you should put more emphasis on your experience. One says that a resume should never be more than one page in length and that it should always be on white paper; another says that two pages is acceptable and that colored paper has the advantage of attracting attention.

We are not going to take sides on the many arguments about what is the best content or the proper form. That is a personal matter in two ways: you, as the writer and subject of your resume, need to reflect your own preferences; and you can be sure that the readers of the resume will react in terms of their own personal preferences. As we suggested earlier there are two primary rules: know yourself, and learn as much as you can about the preferences and prejudices of the one(s) who will read your resume.

We suggest the following approach to resolving the problems of knowing what you are inclined towards and predicting what the readers will be looking for. First, make a list of all the possible variations in form and content of resumes that you can imagine. Treat this as a list of *questions* about resumes. Don't worry at this point about either your answers or the answers that you imagine the readers of your resume will prefer. Both of those decisions will come in the second part of this exercise. The most important thing is to get as broad a view as you can of all the possible ways to prepare a resume.

If you are working with a group you can expand your research net even further and develop a large and very useful pool of questions before you get started on answers.

If you are working alone, go to a library (or, better yet, a career center with its own specialized collection of resources, or the internet with its plentiful sources) and review articles and books that have been written on resumes. Joyce Lain Kennedy's book *Resume for Dummies* continues, in its fourth edition, to be a definitive guide to this subject.

Part 2 of this exercise is to pick and choose from all the advice you have collected in Part 1. In addition to getting a long list of possible combinations of content and form, you will also find it very useful to get some actual resumes and make yourself a display of them. This will give you a chance to see how some of the advice you have collected really looks when it is put into practice. Again, an advantage of working in a group is that you can share the assignment of gathering a variety of actual resumes.

After you have gone this far it probably won't be difficult to decide what you like and don't like about various kinds of resumes. Your eyes will tell you whether you prefer white paper, or "off white" or some color. And you will get a feeling for what kinds of descriptions of skills, experience and personal data appeal to you. When you can't decide between one arrangement and another you can try out both of them. It is a good idea to experiment with different combinations until you get one or more that you like.

It is more difficult, of course, to determine what the potential resume readers will like. You may get some consensus as you discuss the various questions with others. You may even want to interview someone who regularly reads resumes. In the end, however, you will need to settle for your own best guess about what will be most appealing to your resume readers. The only thing that is really certain is that they will have as many different ideas as you discovered when you drew up the list of questions for Part 1 of this exercise.

The Short Distance from "Excellent" to "Unacceptable"

One of our students (we'll call her Lisa Jones) was a secretary and wanted to move up to an administrative position. She wrote a resume, sent it to an employer who was advertising for an executive position, was interviewed and landed the job — at a significant raise in pay.

Was it a good resume? Well, it worked. It looked nice. We used it as an example for students in subsequent classes. There were no negative comments for a couple of years. Then we got a surprise. Lisa's resume was included with about 40 others displayed around the walls of the classroom. Students browsed around the display choosing good and bad examples of content and form. Surprise! Lisa's resume was on more than half of the "bad" lists. This particular group of students reacted negatively to several items:

1. Lisa referred to herself as "generally considered to be attractive".

2. She included as evidence of her excellent job performance the fact that her present employers had gotten into the habit of referring to the "bad old days BLJ." (BLJ meaning "before Lisa Jones".)

3. Besides these questions about the content of her resume the students also objected to its form: written as a narrative, paragraph style; and more than two pages long.

Overall, the class put Lisa's resume at the bottom of their list. They were very surprised when they learned that she had used it successfully to move up from a secretarial to a management position. They raised an interesting question: Was Lisa hired *because* of the resume, or in spite of it? What other factors may have been relevant? Was there a wild card in the deck?

Answer: We don't know. And, we don't really know what makes a good resume. It depends very much on who reads it.

The final part of this exercise is the first draft of your own resume. We have not included a model, sample or suggested format. Your resume is a personal product. It represents you. You should be its author and designer. (It is a good idea to avoid the temptation of hiring someone else to do it. Many employers say that they can spot the "store bought" resumes immediately, and discard them.)

Finally, you may want to have more than one resume, perhaps a general one and then some "targeted" ones aimed at specific employers. And, in the long run, no matter what kind of resume you develop, or how many you have, you will always be revising it (or them) to keep current with your growth and success in your career. After you have finished these two exercises prepare a draft resume and ask for comments from several people.

Worksheet for Exercise 14.1: Questions about the Form and the Content of Resumes

Instructions: Remember that these are *questions* rather than answers. For example, we start you off with "length?" as a question, rather than suggesting a common answer such as "resumes should only be one page in length." And we start you off with "references?" as a relevant question about the content of your resume, rather than suggesting a rule such as "Don't list references on your resume."

From your reading and discussions make as long a list as you can on both form and content. Once you have a complete list of possible questions, you can begin to decide what answers are right for you.

Worksheet for Exercise 14.2: Answers: What Kind of Resume Do You Prefer for Yourself?

Instructions: Review the list of questions in *Exercise 14.1*. Look at some sample resumes to see how others have answered those questions. Decide which answers seem best to you and make a list on this worksheet of the things you want to have in your resume and the way you want it to look. A few categories are suggested below, but they are in no particular order, and you should feel free to use them or not as you prefer.

Questions about Resume Form

(e.g., Length? Color of Paper?)

_____

_____

_____

_____

Questions about Resume Content

(e.g., References? Lists of Jobs Held?)

_____

_____

_____

_____

_____

_____

_____

_____

Answers about Resume Form

Length _____ Type style _____

Color and Quality of Paper _____

Other _____

_____

_____

_____

_____

Answers about Resume Content

Personal Data _____
_____
_____

Objectives _____
_____
_____

Skills _____
_____
_____
_____
_____

Experience _____
_____
_____
_____
_____
_____

Hobbies _____
_____

Other _____
_____
_____
_____
_____

EXERCISE 15
Preparing for Your Job Interviews

When we introduced the subject of job-seeking we suggested that there are only two real rules: know yourself; and know as much as you can about those who will be evaluating you.

You have made a lot of progress on the first of these rules, know yourself. You know your values, your skills, your learning style, and your history — both your formal education and your experience that you described in *Exercise 13*. Now, in *Exercise 15*, you will add two more vital advantages: a survey of what prospective employers are looking for in job interviews; and some practice in giving them what they want.

What do employers look for in job interviews? You have already asked this question about resumes. What you found out was that there are almost as many answers as there are employers. The same thing tends to be true about job interviews — although there are a few more "rules" that are generally accepted. Before you try to decide what you think are the most important do's and don'ts about interviewing make yourself a long list of all the "rules" that other people have suggested. Again, Joyce Lain Kennedy's book *Interviews* is a very good and accessible resource for these standards.

There are hundreds of books and articles filled with ideas about what works and what doesn't in job interviews. Read as much as you can and record the rules in the do's and don'ts columns of *Exercise 15.1* on the next page. You can add some valuable insights to your list by actually interviewing experienced interviewers and asking them what they think is most important. If you are working in a group you will be able to collect a wider range of ideas.

Worksheet for Exercise 15.1: Possible Do's and Don'ts about Job Interviews

Instructions: Remember that this list of possible do's and don'ts is a list of *suggestions,* and is not a list of your own personal conclusions about what is the best way to approach a job interview. For example, we start you off with some contradictory suggestions about how to dress for an interview, and equally contradictory suggestions about what to discuss in the interview. We recommend that you wait until you get to Worksheet 15.4 to decide which of these suggestions you want to follow. In the meantime, make as long a list as you can of all the possible do's and don'ts that you can identify from your reading and your discussions.

Possible Do's and Don'ts about Job Interviews

Always dress conservatively.

Dress in the way in which you feel most comfortable.

Never mention salary because they will think you are only interested in money.

Be sure to talk about salary, otherwise they will think you don't care how much you would be paid.

Don't smoke, even if you are offered a cigarette.

It is o.k. to smoke if the interviewer does.

_____
_____
_____
_____
_____
_____
_____
_____
_____
_____
_____
_____
_____

Worksheet for Exercise 15.2: The Common Questions in Job Interviews

While you are researching the do's and don'ts you will also run across many lists of "The Most Common Questions Asked in Job Interviews." These lists can be very useful to you as you prepare for your own interviews. Of course, the kinds of questions asked will vary with the kind of job you are seeking. You will want to make a separate list of these job-specific questions. But for basic preparation you will want to pay a great deal of attention to those common questions that may be asked in any interview. You will find that experts vary in their estimates of what are the most common questions, or the most important ones. Don't worry about finding the perfect list. But do collect at least a dozen or so of the most common questions for which you should know your own answers. In Worksheet 15.2 we start you off with a few that are found on almost every list.

Instructions: From your reading and discussions, make a list of all the common questions that you think prospective employers might ask during a job interview. We have listed four of the most common questions on the following page.

The Most Common Questions Asked in Job Interviews

Tell me about yourself.

What are your greatest strengths?

What are your worst weaknesses?

Have you ever been fired from a job?

Massaging the Data

After you have collected a list of do's and don'ts you will need to think about each one thoroughly. Just as the resume is a personal document, so is the job interview a very personal process. You cannot become somebody else. But, you do need to decide what kind of appearance you think is appropriate. You need to decide what image you want to project in an interview, and how you are most comfortable doing it.

If you are in a class, you will find it useful to break into small groups and discuss the important do's and don'ts of interviewing. When each group has made its list and presented it you will have all the ingredients you need for a valuable discussion of interviewing techniques. Then you can complete your own personal list of the interviewing strengths on which you think you need to concentrate your preparation. Jot down on page 136 the things that you think are the most important to remember, and to practice, in order to improve your chances for success in future job interviews.

Worksheet for Exercise 15.3: Preparation for Successful Job Interviews

Instructions: As you review *Exercises 15.1* and *15.2*, make a list on this worksheet of the things you need to do, and the skills you need to practice to ensure successful interviews. For example: researching the employer, planning your questions, practicing such things as maintaining good eye contact and good posture, etc.

Things to Do and Practice for a Successful Job Interview

Interviewing Practice

Now that you know what you think are the most important interviewing techniques it is time to practice using them. There are at least three good ways to sharpen your skills:

1. The most effective preparation is a videotaped interview. Many career centers offer this service. And you can do it on your own if you have a VCR and somebody to help you. As you respond to some of the common questions that you identified in *Exercise 15.2* the videotape will record your performance as it would be seen by a job interviewer. Afterwards you have a chance to see yourself as the interviewer will be seeing you. This will give you a chance to work on any adjustments to your style that you think are necessary to improve your performance.

2. Whether or not you can arrange to be videotaped, you can get some valuable practice with mock interviews. Once again there is an advantage to being in a group. You can interview each other, using the list of common questions. After each interview (or after each question) you can share reactions and get some valuable tips about your strengths and weaknesses as an interviewee.

3. Finally, you may find it helpful to rehearse alone — perhaps in front of a mirror — responding to the common questions. While this can be a valuable experience it lacks one vital and realistic ingredient: the interviewer.

Ultimately, of course, real interviews are the very best way to develop your skills. Planning ahead (as you have been doing in this Exercise) is not the only good rule. You should also develop the habit of evaluating your performance after each interview. Ask yourself: What worked? What didn't? What mistakes did you make? What can you do to improve? Often the interviewer will be willing to help you with this evaluation. Whether you get the job or not, don't be afraid to ask interviewers to share with you their thoughts about your strengths and weaknesses in the interview.

Suggestion: You will find that *Exercise 16, The Lifelong Learning Log* (p. 145) is an excellent way of evaluating your interview experience.

Worksheet for Exercise 15.4: Interview Practice and Rehearsal Plans

Instructions: Note on the following worksheet all of the preparatory activities you plan to undertake before going to a job interview.

Interviewing Practice

Videotaped practice interviews
In a career center, class or at home

_____
_____
_____
_____

Other mock interviews

_____
_____
_____
_____

Practicing alone

_____
_____
_____
_____

Other

_____
_____
_____
_____
_____

Job Success and Career Success

Success in your career will be built on a series of successes in your jobs. You may get the job you want as a result of a successful interview. And you will have a successful interview if you:

- know what you want — *Task One*

- know your strengths and weaknesses — *Task Two*

- know how to match your values and skills to jobs and careers — *Task Three*

- have a lifelong learning plan for "bridging the gap" between the skills you have and the skills you need — *Task Four*

- develop and practice effective job-seeking skills — *Task Five.*

You can accomplish each of these five tasks. In each one of them, you can even exceed your own expectations. We are confident that the Tasks and Exercises in this workbook will help you to earn a lifetime of career success!

CONCLUSION
Learning to Learn

Throughout this workbook we have emphasized the unique importance of learning how to learn. It is the master key to insuring your continued career success.

In the "old days" it may not have been so. One chose a career path, went to school to prepare for it, graduated, went to work in the career, and later retired. That has been changed. Change is, in fact, the only thing that is constant with regard to work. Without effective lifelong learning habits you cannot expect to be successful in your career.

Among the vital ingredients of success that are constantly changing are:

- *what* you need to learn;
- *how* you can learn most efficiently;
- *when* you need to learn.

EXERCISE 16
Lifelong Learning Logs: Monitors of Your Career Success

It is no wonder that employers rate "the ability to learn" very high on their lists of criteria for hiring and promotion. It is also no surprise that career success comes most generously to those who learn most effectively.

We conclude this workbook with an exercise designed to keep you in constant touch with changes in your learning needs. Incorporating the Learning Log into your daily career routine is like taking out a "career success insurance policy." A good learning log will help you with each important element of successful learning:

- recognizing new learning needs as they arise;

- discovering and using new learning activities and helpful resources;

- evaluating your progress.

There is not much value in doing *Exercise 16* just once. It is meant to be repeated whenever a useful learning incident occurs. On the other hand, it is not realistic to expect that you will sit down and log every time you run across an opportunity to learn something. What we recommend is that you begin by actually writing a log each time a particularly appropriate learning opportunity arises. Perhaps once a week for a while. Later, as you develop the habit of analyzing your learning experiences you will be able to complete this exercise just by making a few notes and thinking about them. Eventually this kind of valuable analysis will become an almost automatic routine response to daily events.

There are four steps to effective log writing:

1. *describing* an incident that offers an effective learning opportunity

2. *analyzing* the incident

3. *considering alternative actions* that might have altered the outcome

4. *planning* future activities, both traditional and experiential, that will extend your learning

Enter your responses to these four items on the worksheet. For maximum benefit you should share your log with one or more persons who know you and/or the situation well. The more evaluation you receive, the more accurate your analysis will be and the more effectively the learning outcomes will contribute to your career success.

Worksheet for Exercise 16: The Lifelong Learning Log

Instructions:

1. DESCRIBE an incident that you experienced (or observed someone else experiencing). The incident should involve a skill that you want to develop. Your description should answer the "who, what, when, where" questions and provide all the data you need for a complete analysis.

2. ANALYZE the incident. Answer the "why" question. What caused the incident to have a positive or negative outcome?

3. CONSIDER THE ALTERNATIVES. If you had behaved differently, how might the outcome have been changed? Identify all of the alternative ways in which this incident could have been handled and list the advantages and disadvantages of each.

4. PLAN now how you will apply your learning from this incident. Does it suggest some new and important learning objectives? Can you identify some opportunities to experiment or practice some skills? Is there some way in which this incident can help you to become a better learner?

The Lifelong Learning Log
make several copies of this worksheet

Describe an incident

_____
_____
_____
_____

Analyze the incident

_____
_____
_____
_____

Consider the alternatives

_____
_____
_____

Your plan

_____
_____
_____
_____
_____

APPENDICES
Helpful Resources

There are many different kinds of resources available to help you with each element of career success. This is a partial list of some helpful publications and organizations.

Job Search Strategies

Joyce Lain Kennedy is a widely respected author whose syndicated CAREERS NOW column for Tribune Media Service appears in more than 100 newspapers and websites. She has written three of the books in the "For Dummies" series published by Wiley: *Resumes for Dummies, Cover Letters for Dummies,* and *Job Interviews for Dummies.*

International Jobs and Careers

Eric Kocher is the author of *International Jobs: Where They Are and How To Get Them, Fifth Edition*

(Perseus Publishing, 1998) For twenty years this book has been an authoritative guide to launching and enhancing an international career. The updated edition of the book provides all the information job seekers need to navigate the increasingly complex 21st century international job market. This guide contains website addresses and advice on how to effectively use the internet in a global job search.

Foreign Policy Association is a nongovernmental, nonprofit educational organization founded in 1918 to educate Americans about the significant international issues that influence their lives. The FPA offers substantial support to students wishing to study foreign policy through its Great Decisions education program, and provides free online newsletters with a wealth of current information. It also provides postings of international study opportunities for high school as well as college students. The FPA offers an internet posting of Global Jobs by subscription that includes internships, and job and volunteer opportunities. You can contact the FPA at 212-481-8100 or write to: Foreign Policy Association, 470 Park Avenue South, New York, NY 10016. Website: www.fpa.org.

Computerized Career Programs

Several computerized programs to guide the user through the career search process are available. Two excellent national programs with proven track records are briefly described below.

SIGI PLUS (System of Interactive Guidance

and Information) is produced by the Educational Testing Service in Princeton, NJ. Its interactive programs are made available to career centers, institutions, libraries and others for use by adult learners as well as pre-career young people. This career planning software program includes values clarification exercises and other information to assist users in selecting careers compatible with their values and skills. The program also includes links to educational and career planning resources to match occupations with educational experience. For further information write to Educational Testing Service, Rosedale Road, Princeton NJ 08541 or call 609-921-9000. Visit SIGI's website at www.ets.org/sigi for valuable information on many testing instruments used in the academic and professional arena today. There are regional, as well as worldwide offices.

DISCOVER is produced by ACT in Iowa City, IA. It provides a developmental guidance process and detailed information to help users make career and educational decisions—whether they are planning immediate employment, vocational training, college or military service. The system also provides complete, current databases of occupations, college majors, schools and training institutions, financial aid and scholarships and military options. There is now an internet version of the program that can be progressed through with a password system that will maintain a personal record for users, and is offered through licensed organizations such as schools, libraries and career centers. For information call 319-337-1031 or email: discover@act.org. Website: www.act.org

Learning

David Kolb's *Learning Style Inventory* (LSI3, updated 1999) is based on the theory of experiential learning. The LSI3 measures an individual's strengths and weaknesses as a learner. The Inventory can be completed online, or on paper. For a very good informational site, visit www.hayresourcesdirect.haygroup.com or contact Hay Resources Direct, 116 Huntington Avenue, Boston MA 02116, or phone 800-729-8074.

Lois Lamdin's book *Earn College Credit For What You Know, 3rd Edition,* continues to be an excellent resource for information on Prior Learning Assessment (PLA) and the portfolio method of documenting 'learning from experience'. The book also contains useful information for adult learners on life and career planning, choosing the right school, and surviving and thriving in college. The book is published by the Council for Adult and Experiential Learning (CAEL) and can be ordered from Kendall-Hunt at 800-228-0810 or at www.kendallhunt.com

Prior Learning Assessment: A Guidebook to American Institutional Practices, by Zucker, Johnson, & Flint and also published by CAEL gives extensive information detailing the methods that more than 1,000 US colleges and universities use to do PLA to award credit, including both national and local examinations, evaluation of non-college instructional programs offered by the military and by corporations, as well as individualized portfolio methods. Search www.kendallhunt.com for both books by title or author.

Professional Organizations

Council for Adult and Experiential Learning (CAEL) is an international association composed of colleges and universities, corporations, unions, government agencies, organizations and individuals. Its mission is to expand lifelong learning opportunities for adults and to advance experiential learning and its assessment.

For users of this workbook CAEL offers various kinds of helpful resources including:

Publications (such as Lois Lamdin's book, *Earn College Credit For What You Know*, described on pg. 149) are available to help educators and students to evaluate their prior experiential learning for possible credit. CAEL publications are available through Kendall-Hunt, 800-228-0810 or on the web at www.kendallhunt.com.

The Employee Potential Program, a unique capability assessment process developed by CAEL and Charles River Consulting, Inc. The Program provides both unemployed and employed workers with valuable knowledge about their transferable capabilities and motivates them to become involved in job and career counseling, education and training programs, job placement services and other assistance available to them.

Research by CAEL promotes effective prior learning assessment practice and monitors institutional use of PLA in higher education.

Membership in CAEL offers institutions, organizations, and individuals the benefit of ongoing updates of CAEL activities and discounts on its books and monographs. CAEL members also receive discounts for registration at its international conference (usually held in mid-November). For information on membership and available resources write to 55 East Monroe, Suite 1930, Chicago, IL 60603, 312-499-2600. Website: www.cael.org.

ALLIANCE: An Association for Alternative Degree Programs for Adults is an association of individuals and organizations committed to helping institutions of higher education develop and sustain learning environments and programs for adults. The primary mission of the Alliance is to serve professionals and institutions offering alternative undergraduate and graduate degree programs for adults by fostering the exchange of ideas, supporting the professional development of members, and serving as an advocate for adult students and alternative degree programs for adults. An annual conference, co-sponsored by the American Council on Education (ACE), is held in the autumn every year. A volunteer board of directors publishes a newsletter for members and maintains a network of professionals available for consultation and program review activities. For further information contact Roberta Hartmann, Alliance Director for Membership, Sinclair Community College, 444 W. Third Street, Dayton, OH 45402. Website: www.ahea.org.

National Society for Experiential Education (NSEE) is a nonprofit membership association of educators, businesses, and community leaders committed to all forms of experiential learning—whether they happen in the classroom, workplace, or community. NSEE also serves as a national resource center for the development and improvement of experiential education programs nationwide. NSEE supports the use of learning through experience for: intellectual development, cross-cultural and global awareness, civic and social responsibility, ethical development, career exploration and personal growth. The organization offers professional members ongoing development which includes an annual conference, publications and research. National Society for Experiential Education, 9001 Braddock Road, Suite 380, Springfield, VA 22151, 703-426-4268/800-803-4170. Website: www.nsee.org.

Cooperative Education & Internship Association is a leader in providing professional development and resources to practitioners in the field of cooperative education. The original mission of the organization as envisioned by its founders in 1963 is carried out through an expanding number of training activities, an annual national conference, and support and encouragement for on-going research and publications. It publishes a monthly newsletter and a quarterly journal. For information on membership and other resources write to: CEIA, Inc., 4190 S. Highland Drive, Suite 211, Salt Lake City, UT 84124, 800-824-0449. Website: www.ceainc.org.

National Commission for Cooperative Education (NCCE) is dedicated to promoting cooperative education throughout the US. The Commission works with colleges, employers and policy makers to expand this successful work and learning program through national advocacy, executive outreach, public awareness, student and parent response and through research and educational programs. The website very clearly defines for students and their parents, the co-op model of education which combines classroom studies with paid productive employment. For more information contact 360 Huntington Avenue, 384CP, Boston, MA 02115, 617-373-3770. Website: www.co-op.edu.

American Council on Education (ACE) functions primarily to provide a forum for the discussion of major issues related to higher education. For nearly 60 years, ACE's Military Programs department has been translating military courses and occupational learning outcomes into academic credit. The goal is to help servicemembers and veterans use their military knowledge and experience to further their education and advance their careers. The Council publishes and makes available online a very useful publication that is updated every two years called *Guide to the Evaluation of Educational Experiences in the Armed Services* which contains information for those seeking to receive credit for their military training. Contact: Military Programs, One Dupont Circle NW, Suite 250, Washington DC 20036, 202-939-9475. Website: www.acenet.edu/calec/military.

About the Author

Urban Whitaker was born in Kansas in 1924 and grew up in Southern California. He earned a B.A. in Political Science at Occidental College in 1947. He attended Midshipmen's School at Columbia University in New York during World War II and then served as a Naval Reserve Officer on combat duty in the Western Pacific. Following the war he studied language and culture in Beijing, China in 1947-48, then completed his doctoral studies at the University of Washington in Seattle. He served two more years of combat duty in the Navy during the Korean War before completing his Ph.D. in Far Eastern Studies and Political Science in 1954.

Dr. Whitaker joined the faculty at San Francisco State University where he served as a Professor of International Relations and in various administrative roles from 1954 until his retirement in 1995. In 1960-61 Dr. Whitaker spent a year at the United Nations as a Research Fellow for Columbia University. He interviewed representatives of all the member nations and published several articles about the question of Chinese Representation. He served for many years on the national boards of directors of the United Nations Association and the Commission to Study the Organization of Peace. In 1964 he wrote *Politics and Power: A Text in International Law*.

While serving as Dean of Undergraduate Studies for a decade in the 60's and 70's he became a founding member of The Council for Adult and Experiential Learning (CAEL) and was active in the National Society for Experiential Learning (NSEE). He served on the Boards of Directors of both organizations and has written numerous books and articles on experiential learning and career development. His book *Assessing Learning: Standards, Principles and Procedures,* published by CAEL in 1989 became the standard work on quality assurance in the field of experiential learning. He has been a consultant and workshop leader at many colleges and universities in North America and abroad, and has served on many accreditation teams.

After joining the Faculty Early Retirement Program in 1979, Dr. Whitaker taught courses in Career Development and International Careers at San Francisco State University until his retirement in 1995.

As a consultant on experiential learning, Dr. Whitaker has been invited to universities in New Zealand, Canada and South Africa. In 1994 he was awarded the Morris T. Keeton Medal for outstanding contributions in experiential and adult learning. In October of 2001 he was presented with an honorary Doctorate of Humane Letters by Thomas Edison State College, in recognition of his 13 years of service on the faculty of the National Institute on the Assessment of Experiential Learning.

Urban Whitaker and his wife, Jean, live in the San Francisco Bay Area.